GOD'S

GENTLE

WHISPER

Denise George

GOD'S GENTLE WHISPER

DEVELOPING A RESPONSIVE HEART TO GOD

A LONGING HEART HEARS

DENISE GEORGE

Copyright © Denise George

10 9 8 7 6 5 4 3 2 1

ISBN 1-84550-236-1
ISBN 978-1-84550-236-2

Published in 2007
by
Christian Focus Publications,
Geanies House, Fearn, Tain, Ross-shire,
IV20 1TW, Scotland, UK

www.christianfocus.com

Cover design by Moose77.com

Printed and bound by
Nørhaven Paperback A/S, Denmark

CONTENTS

SECTION I: THE WAITING HEART

1. Standing on the Mountain: The Secret Place 11
2. The Seeking Heart 23
3. Waiting for the Lord to Pass By 35

SECTION II: THE LISTENING HEART

4. Listening for the Father's Voice 51
5. Earthquake, Wind, and Fire 67
6. God's Gentle Whisper 81

SECTION III: THE RESPONSIVE HEART

7. Standing at the Mouth of the Cave 91
8. The Servant's Heart 107
9. The Shepherd's Heart 119

For Deeper Understanding of Scripture 133
More About Elijah 135

Dedication

For
my special friends who have inspired
and encouraged me in so many ways:
Dr. Warren Wiersbe and Mrs. Betty Wiersbe

The LORD said, 'Go out and stand on the mountain in the presence of the LORD, for the LORD is about to pass by.'

Then a great and powerful wind tore the mountains apart and shattered the rocks before the LORD, but the LORD was not in the wind. After the wind there was an earthquake, but the LORD was not in the earthquake. After the earthquake came a fire, but the LORD was not in the fire. And after the fire came *a gentle whisper*. When Elijah heard it, he pulled his cloak over his face and went out and stood at the mouth of the cave.

(1 Kings 19:11-13)

Before you begin reading *God's Gentle Whisper*, please take a few minutes, find a comfortable quiet place, and read the fascinating story of the prophet Elijah, found in 1 Kings 17, 18, and 19.

My heartfelt thank you to all those wonderful people who made this book possible, Willie MacKenzie, Editorial Manager and his colleague Annella MacDonald.

As a Christian woman, I believe our life's goal is to know God, to love God, and to serve God.

We come to know God, to love God, and to serve God through prayer.

But prayer is not only speaking our words to Him.

Prayer is also finding a quiet place, and with the ears of seeking hearts, waiting and listening for God's gentle whisper to us.

For when we learn to listen with the ears of our hearts, we come to know God.

When we hear His gentle whisper, we come to love God.

And when to His whisper our listening hearts respond, we prepare to serve God.

May God richly bless you as you journey through the pages of this book.

Denise George

SECTION I

THE WAITING HEART

ONE

STANDING ON THE MOUNTAIN:

THE SECRET PLACE

While my young son plays quietly in the next room, I sit beside my grandmother's bed and hold her trembling hand. Beneath the layers of handmade quilts, I see the frail woman I call 'Mama,' the woman I have loved dearly for more than three decades.

Alice Crane Williams, my beloved grandmother – Mama – is dying. I cannot imagine life without her.

She is a simple woman who has suffered a lifetime of sickness and surgery. In her 80 years, she has never written a check, never driven a car, and never worked outside her home.

She would not rate very high on the world's yardstick of accomplishment. Yet, I know few women who have accomplished more. She has lived a long life in step with her Lord, empowered by the Holy Spirit, devoted to discipleship. Her spiritual impact on others has been profound. As my spiritual mother, she has left an indelible fingerprint of love and grace and beauty on my life.

A Welcome Haven

A storm brews outside her home, the white gabled house I have known since my birth. Dark clouds appear and are followed by bouts of thunder and lightning. The winds begins snapping off young trees at their roots and tossing them into the yard.

I expect to hear my son scream out with fear as I glance out the window into nature's unexpected chaos. Yet, however frightening the scene beyond these walls, inside we feel safe, secure, unafraid, and very much loved. The house is a welcome haven from the turmoil all around us.

Mama and I are not alone in the room where I so often slept as a child. For within me is nestled one still in development, one who will carry on my grandmother's name. My unborn daughter, Alyce, remains peaceful in her secret place beneath my heart. It is as if she somehow senses the preciousness of this moment for Mama and me, our moment of timelessness, our moment of unspoken prayer together in our own secret place.

Will Mama live to look upon the face of her new great-granddaughter, her only namesake? I wonder as greater darkness and the threat of more severe storms shadow the room.

I already seem to know the answer.

No, she won't. Mama will close her eyes and cease her breathing just ten days before Alyce will open her eyes and take her first breath of life.

This is our last meeting on this earth. Our final face-to-face farewell. And with the birth of my daughter so close at hand, I won't be able to travel the long distance to her funeral. We both sense we will meet again only in the promised life hereafter. What does one say or do or think at the 'final meeting'? I have never known a time without my grandmother. Her loving arms welcomed me into this world, surrounded me as a child, and nurtured me to adulthood. I cannot imagine life without her tender, wise counsel.

So many times I have made the 300-mile trek to sit by my grandmother's side. Like little girls at a slumber party, we have talked and giggled and dreamed about the future. And how the minutes flew! We looked at our watches as if staring hard enough at them would make time show down. But, alas, each time, the sun rose, I rolled up my sleeping bag, packed my pajamas, said my thank-yous and goodbyes, and returned to my busy world far away from Mama's world.

Mama and I have loved our many times of nonstop conversation. But today, in Mama's short meantime between physical life and physical death, in this time of remembering and quiet waiting, we do not speak. We need no words. And in this secret place, our paradise away from the thundering world outside, we sense the presence of Another who remembers quietly and waits in this precious moment with us.

*

There are times in our lives so deep, so precious, so mysterious, so near to the core of our hearts, that words only hinder our communion. Thus it is with prayer. Our hearts can be so full of love or pain or gratitude or fear that our very silence overflows with meaning beyond the limited capability of words. We express ourselves instead with the prayer that pours forth from a touched heart, a heart so sensitive to its own beat that words would be bumbling.

'The fewer words the better prayer,' said reformer Martin Luther.

On this night, this storm-raged night when death glares at us from down the hall, I would agree with Dr. Luther. Words need be sparse. Our clasped hands, smiling eyes, and grateful memories of a life lived side by side, say more than we ever could with verbal words. In fact, words would make a clumsy stab at what our hearts so eloquently express.

God's Whisper

'But thou, when thou prayest, enter into thy closet, and when thou hast shut thy door, pray to thy Father which is in secret....' (Matt. 6:6 KJV.)

'Thy Father which is in secret....' Mama has spent much time in closet-prayer secreted with the Father. In fact, her entire life has been a prayer. More than anyone else, Mama has taught me the value and beauty of a secret place and a prayer of waiting and listening to the still, small voice that whispers within the prayer-closet walls.

One of my favorite authors, C. S. Lewis, believed that 'God whispers to us in our pleasures, ... but shouts in our pain: it is His megaphone,' he writes, 'to rouse a deaf world.'[1]

Dare I disagree with C. S. Lewis?

I would reverse the order. For I believe it is in our times of pleasure that God must shout and rouse our deaf ears. Pleasure so often dulls our sense of need for God. Truly, it is in our pain that He need only whisper. For in our pain the deaf ears of our hearts are unstopped, waiting, listening, hanging onto the comfort of His every word. Pain, the Great Teacher, can break our hearts and cause us to contemplate deeply humankind's most pondered question: 'Why, Lord, why?' There is but one Theologian who knows the answer. Thus, to Him, we turn our hearts and yearn for deeper understanding into the great mystery of life.

Waiting. Watching. Listening. There are many wonderful and beautiful ways to pray, to communicate with the Father. But it is the prayer that waits and watches, the prayer that perks the ears of our hearts to strain and to listen expectantly for God's gentle whisper that compels me to record it. For this

---

1. C. S. Lewis, The Problem with Pain (London, England: Fontana, 1940), p. 93.

waiting, this 'standing under, in active strength, enduring till the answer comes,'[2] describes prayer at its richest.

I have discovered an abundant love for this type of prayer, the prayer of the waiting heart. Perhaps you, too, have discovered its surprising beauty and lasting afterglow.

I used to think of waiting as a passive activity. I have felt time wasting as I've stood in long, grocery check-out lines, bank lines, cafeteria lines, and post office lines. I loathe that kind of waiting where I must persist staring into space with an empty mind wandering. But waiting in prayer is nothing like waiting in line. It is far from a passive activity.

When God's great and beloved prophet, Elijah, waited for God on the side of the mountain, he did not passively sit or lie or lounge in his waiting. He had no blank stare and wandering empty mind. Elijah stood on the mountain, actively waiting, his eyes alert and watchful, his ears perked and eager to detect even the hint of God's voice. Longing, straining, yearning to hear from God.

Over the past years, Elijah has taught me much about how to pray this way. Elijah and Mama.

Mama's Secret Place

Oh, that I could know God as Elijah and Mama knew him!

On a cool spring morning, long before the pet rooster summoned us to rise, I looked from the kitchen window, beyond the tall old hickory nut trees, to the gardens that bloomed in bounty each year. Mama's flower gardens. Mama's secret place to meet the Lord.

I am sure her gardens brought more than one passerby to prayer. So lovely they lined the small farm's edge. People often

---

2. Oswald Chambers, *If You Will Ask* (Grand Rapids, MI: Discovery House Publishers, 1958), p. 36.

stopped and admired them for a few rare moments of hushed beauty. And there in the midst of dew-laden blooms, Mama slowly walked. At times she lingered, her lips moving in silent prayer. Most times, however, her lips were still. She touched a treasured rose, and then with eyes moist from an overflowing and grateful heart, she simply looked towards the heavens and smiled.

Mama needed no words to commune with her Father. For they had walked through the gardens many times together, for many years, their hearts beating as one in perfect peace, tranquility and communion.

My friend, do you have a secret place, a place where you go alone to wait and watch and listen for the Lord? A place where you go faithfully to know your Father more intimately?

God is a God who wants to be known.[3] We wait, we watch, we listen, and God rewards our seeking with knowledge of Himself.[4] Dr. J. I. Packer, in his book *Knowing God* writes that the greatest gift God gives us is the gift of knowing Him.[5] Imagine! We can actually know the one who created us in our 'secret place,' the one who knew us in our mother's womb long before we drew our first breath of air and opened our eyes to His glorious creation.

I have had many secret places over the years, places where I have spent quiet precious moments with the Lord. Some places were lovely to the eye and peaceful to the heart.

I remember the little private spot hidden by trees on a remote tall mountain in Rüschlikon, Switzerland, the 'village of roses.' It became my secret place of worship for almost a year while my family and I lived and worked in Switzerland.

---

3. Hebrews 1:1-2.

4. Hebrews 11:6.

5. J. I. Packer, *Knowing God* (Downers Grover, IL: InterVarsity Press, 1973), pp. 14-15.

I often stood on the side of the mountain in the pine straw nest powered with fresh snow, and tried to absorb the incomprehensible beauty. The emerald and shimmering gold Lake Zurich laid directly below me, the forests of snow-laden evergreens surrounded me, and the mighty Alps rose in distant peaks beyond me. It seemed right out of a storybook. I often blinked my eyes to believe the exquisite scenery before me.

On this, my own Elijah's mountain, I stood silently, my mouth agape in awe of the Creator's masterpiece. I believed no place in the world could be more breathtakingly beautiful.

Waiting? Yes.

Watching? Definitely.

Listening? With all the strength I could summon.

There, I waited in my own secret place, with expectation and a seeking heart, waiting for the Lord to pass by.

An Inner City Secret Place

In sharp contrast to Rüschlikon, with its rose petal fragrance lingering in the air, was another of my many secret places: Chelsea, Massachusetts, a dirty, violent, inner city located on the outskirts of Boston, Massachusetts.

It was a far cry from Rüschlikon with its Sleeping Beauty/ Cinderella setting. In storybook language, Chelsea would be more like Alice in Wonderland with its dangerous pathways, unpredictable curves, and its strange assortment of malevolent characters hiding behind every wall. A storm of violence, pain, and suffering rained heavily on the 30,000 Chelsea residents of all colors, ages, and backgrounds, who lived crowded into two square miles of dirty drab city concrete. We did not choose Chelsea. We are drawn to and inspired by mountains and trees and sparkling lakes – quiet, beauty, and serenity. Chelsea was chosen for us by the mission board of our denomination. Chelsea was indeed a mission field. It proved a seven-year missionary experience I will never forget.

Chelsea had no sweet rose fragrance. Its only beauty lived in the innocent and loving faces of those too young to yet be aware of its filth and poverty.

There was the unwed mother with eleven children living in the one-room attic of a four-story apartment building.

There were the alcoholics who lived in the drainage ditches with no food, no friends, no heat, no medical care, and no hope.

There were gangs of teens drinking, drugging, and drifting through the late night streets with no direction, no guidance, no caring families, and no future outside prison walls.

And there were the children – the innocent ones of the concrete city. Children like David, who was placed in an abusive foster home as a baby. David coped with life as no child should ever have to. We tried to adopt David, the five-year-old boy who had never seen a real flower push its way through soil. But we were unsuccessful. We, too, as students, had little in this world – besides love – that we could offer David. I often wonder where he is now, the dark-skinned boy – now a middle-aged man – with bruises on his back and a little round face that seldom smiled.

In Rüschlikon my heart was filled with prayers of thanksgiving for the beauty that surrounded and inspired me. I needed few words to express the gratitude of my heart.

In Chelsea, however, my heart was filled with prayers for others, the crowds of aimless people who tired to survive hard days surrounded by drugs, guns, prostitution, and desolation. I needed few words to express the pain in my heart for the poverty and suffering that surrounded me. Intercessory prayer from my heart repeatedly asked the 'whys' of faith, the hard questions – questions for which I waited and watched and strained to hear the answers.

In Chelsea, my secret place was a ladder-back chair at an enamel-painted table before a window that looked out on filth and vulgar depravity. But however unsettling the view, I found I was drawn much more to wait in prayer at that kitchen table than on that mountain in Rüschlikon, so great was my need to listen for God's voice in the midst of such fear, destitution, and suffering.

God needed no megaphone to rouse my deaf ears. I lived in Chelsea for only a few miserable years. But these people – who ventured rarely into the outside world – would live there forever. In the pain and pity I felt for them, I listened attentively, carefully for His comforting whisper and the answers I needed to hear and to share.

Back Into the Storm

It is time for me to leave my grandmother's quiet bedroom. For the last time, I lean over and lightly kiss her forehead. I would speak one last time to Mama by phone, but I would never see her again on this earth.

'I'll see you *later*, Mama,' are the only words I speak. We look into each other's eyes and we smile. We both know what *later* means. I stand and back slowly out of the room, taking one last mental snapshot to hold in memory throughout my life without her. Through intense physical pain, she keeps the smile on her lips until the loving embrace of our eyes is broken by distance.

As I leave our secret place, I am once again aware of the storm outside. I lift my small son from his playpen, and together we brace the wind and rain and leave the house that will never be the same to me again.

Every heart must have its hush. I am convinced that the waiting prayer is the most difficult to pray. In our lives, it is often much easier *to do* than it is *to be*, to pray with words and song and joyful dance than to wait and listen in sacred solitude. Yet the Lord summons us to go out and stand on our mountaintop, to 'be still, and know that I am God.'[6]

---

6. Psalm 46:10.

My friend, our hearts are forever searching for a quiet place of solitude, a secret place where we alone can prepare ourselves for an encounter with the living Lord. Find your place. Perk your ears. Frequent often your secret place of solitude and prayer.

Questions for Group Study

1. Have you personally known the richness of a spiritual nurturer in your life? If so, describe that person.

   a. What qualities made her/him different from others you loved and respected?

   b. What traits did she/he possess that spoke to you in spiritually-inspiring ways?

   c. How did that person bring you closer to the Lord?

   d. What is the one most important spiritual lesson you learned from your nurturer?

2. What does this sentence mean to you: 'Our hearts can be so full of love or pain or gratitude or fear that our very silence overflows with meaning beyond the limited capability of words'?

   a. Have you ever prayed so deeply from your heart that words only got in your way? Describe the event. What was your life situation when you prayed that particular prayer?

3. Do you agree with Martin Luther: 'The fewer words the better prayer'? If so, please explain why.

4. What does Scripture teach when it states: 'But thou, when thou prayest, enter into thy closet, and when thou hast shut thy door, pray to thy Father which is in secret....'?[7]

   a. Why is it important that we have a secret place to pray, a private prayer-closet?

   b. What is the significance of the statement: 'When thou hast shut thy door....'?

---

7. Matthew 6:6 (KJV).

c. Do you have a secret place of prayer where you and the Father can regularly meet? If so, please describe it.

d. Why do you think a secret place is important to your life of prayer?

5. Do you agree that: 'It is in our times of pleasure that God must shout and rouse our deaf ears,' and that 'It is in our pain that He need only whisper'? If so, why? If not, why?

6. Oswald Chambers describes 'waiting' as 'standing under, in active strength, enduring till the answer comes.' Do you agree or disagree with his definition and why? What does 'waiting' mean to you?

7. Describe your most beautiful secret place. What qualities did it have, or does it now have, that move you most to prayer?

8. Do you agree that 'the waiting prayer' is the most difficult prayer to pray? If so, please explain why.

9. What are your five greatest strengths and your five greatest weaknesses in your pursuit of prayer? Consider listing them and discussing them with your group.

Suggestions for Personal Reflection

Choose a favorite place in your home or garden or office or city park.

· Decide to visit your secret place at least once a day, if not more often.

· Give yourself time to sit quietly and to relax your body and mind.

· Read favorite selections from Scripture to help you focus more fully on the Lord.

· Pour out your heart to God. Keep nothing from Him.

· Then, listen. Listen as He speaks to the depths of your heart.

- Please don't rush your prayer-closet time, for it takes time to settle down and to concentrate on God, His love, His goodness. It takes time to prepare our hearts to hear His whisper.

- Schedule a time when you will be uninterrupted. Think only about God and His presence. Try to keep your thoughts free from distractions. Concentrate on meeting the Lord and listening to His words to you.

Two

The Seeking Heart

Hot, thirsty, and standing on aching feet, the man answers a deluge of questions – life and death questions – shouted to Him from a throng of people. They strain their ears to hear His answers in the push and shove of the sweaty crowd. Like bath sponges thrown into a vast ocean, they absorb all they can hold, yet they still thirst for more.

Lost coins, new wineskins, vines and branches ... what did it all mean?

The preacher has been telling stories and explaining metaphors for hours without a coffee break. Some friends bring Him a burger and fries, but with the horde swarming around Him, demanding His time, He is unable to eat.

His throat is parched and He is bone-tired, His voice cracks and fades into the lakeside wind.

'Speak louder!' the crowd demands. 'Speak louder! We can't hear you!'

He turns and glances to the mountains on the other side of the lake. A voice beckons Him to come, a call more urgent than the clamor of the crowd.

'C'mon.' He motions to His friends. 'Let's find a quiet place to be alone and get some rest.'

'But ... but ...' His disciples say. 'Leave now? Right in the middle of your sermon?! Why, this is the biggest revival we've ever had! We can't just leave!'

While they protest, Jesus simply walks away toward a little boat that will take Him to the mountaintop, the secret place His weary heart seeks, the place where He can rest in the presence of the One who loves Him most – His Father.

Eyes set on the mountain, heart set on a respite, Jesus climbs into the boat and rows to the other side of the lake.

But, He isn't alone for long. The multitudes have followed Him.

'Surprise!' the unexpected mob jumps out at Him and quickly surrounds Him. They demand He finish His sermon.

Jesus rubs His tired eyes, takes a deep breath, and then lifts His head. He looks into the faces of the people who eagerly wait before Him, people with empty eyes and desperate hearts, people dying of spiritual thirst. They are like a herd of sheep wandering aimlessly through life with no guidance, no direction, and no shepherd.

Jesus leans against a rock for support, clears His throat, and parts His sun-baked lips to speak.

'The Kingdom of God is like a mustard seed,' He begins.

His stories last long into the evening. Before the sun disappears behind the mountains, before fatigue folds His legs beneath Him, Jesus will have filled hungry bellies with fish and loaves, and thirsty hearts with fresh Living Water.

He's Lived Here

Jesus knows how it feels to be hot and thirsty and have aching feet. He knows the pressure of having more to do than can be humanly done in a single hour or day. Jesus dealt with the crowds of demanding, critical people who believed of Him the worst and selfishly asked of Him the impossible. He knew time ticking away, the frustrations of ungrateful friends and family. He knew the pain of blistered hands, swollen eyes, and a hurting heart.

He's lived here, here in this stressful, pressure-packed fast-food society that hasn't really changed that much in 2000 years.

How did He endure it? Or, as we would put it in the 21st century, how did He cope? How did He find rest and peace and tranquility and meaning in the midst of a thunder and lightning world? Where was His safe and secure haven when the storms of life gathered fiercely around Him?

On the mountaintop, His secret place, the place where He journeyed to meet His Father. Our Father.

Jesus spent much time on the mountaintops. When the crowds were at their biggest, when the pressures were at their greatest, He simply headed toward the nearest mountain. He made no excuses, He felt no guilt. When He heard His Father's call, He followed.

Right in the middle of a sermon.

He would have no qualms about leaving dirty dishes in the sink, the checkbook unbalanced, the family room floor unvacu-umed. Prayer time with the Father was more important. It was always the first item on His list of priorities.

Don't you just love a person like that, a person who has the courage to exit the ordinary to enter the extraordinary – a quiet, restful moment spent with God?

Think about it. If Jesus so needed to go to the mountaintop to be with the Father, far from the madding crowds, the pressures, the stresses of everyday life and work; if Jesus so needed to retreat, to pray, and to ponder, how much more do you and I need to take that hike!

Often.

Have you been to the mountaintop lately?

A Little Peace and Quiet

Many Christmases ago, my then three-year-old son, Christian, asked me: 'Mommy, what you want for 'Krismas?'

That year, 1985, my husband, Timothy, and I were taking our study/writing sabbatical in Switzerland. It was the best of times, and it was the worst of times. Timothy and I were both under rigid book deadlines, we were both struggling to communicate in Swiss-German, and we were both trying (unsuccessfully) to potty train two preschoolers! We lived on a major four-land highway in an apartment the size of a postage stamp, with 14 other international families – and one washing machine for us all!

What did I want for Christmas? Like the little boy who only wanted his two front teeth, I, too, had only two items on my gift list.

'All I want for Christmas, Christian,' I answered, 'is a little peace and quiet.'

Have you ever felt that way? Have you ever felt like a pitcher of water that has been poured out for others until it is dry?

I have. I find I need a lot of quiet, personal time with my heavenly Father in order to deal with the complexities of life and work and family and friends.

I believe Jesus felt that way, too. In fact, I'm glad He made so many recorded treks to the mountains to rest and to pray. For His constant retreats give us an example to follow. We are allowed to admit that our bodies grow tired and our hearts are in need of a quiet place where we can be alone with our Father. Jesus, Himself, gives us permission to find needed peace and quiet for our weary soul.

We need no excuses to rest.

We need experience no guilt to soothe our soul.

Prayerful peace and quiet is a precious gift that no amount of money can buy. It is a free gift, a gift from God, Himself. And high on the mountaintop, the Father waits for us, gift in hand, waiting to help us unwrap it.

A Wish Granted

Timothy overheard my request for peace and quiet on that Christmas in 1985. Early that Christmas morning, to my surprise, my wish was granted. From my family I received an envelope 'filled with peace and quiet' – a three-day personal prayer retreat anywhere I wanted to go. Timothy would deal with the preschoolers and the potty-training, and I would spend some time with the Lord.

I chose the quietest place in all of Europe, a large 12th-century stone monastery at the top of a mountain in Kappal, Switzerland. With the exception of a few devoted nuns, the monastery had been deserted centuries ago. I spent those days and nights in silence, communing only with God and with the contented brown and white cows that quietly chewed cud on the hillside.

During the day, I hiked the mountain trails, stopping to touch tender snow-dusted pine needles on lakeside evergreens and running my fingers across the smooth worn surfaces of roadside rocks. At night, I lay very still in my small monk's room and listened to the soft distant chime of Swiss cowbells. I closed my eyes and tried to imagine all the many people who, for hundreds of years, had also waited quietly, prayerfully, in this place. At times, I even thought I heard the swish of a long black robe worn by some ancient monk as he passed silently through the sacred halls.

For three days and three nights I prayed. So as not to break the welcomed stream of silence, I prayed with words only from my heart. It was as if God and I walked together up those mountain trails, hand in hand, in peace and long-awaited rest.

'As a hart longs for flowing streams, so longs my soul for thee, O God,' writes a psalmist with a seeking heart. 'My soul thirsts for God, for the living God. When shall I come and behold the face of God? (Ps. 42:1-2 RSV).

Perhaps the ancient psalmist shares with us some eternal plea for solitude and silence. Deep deep within us, is that not the cry each heart yearningly expresses?

Some years later, St. Augustine would phrase it another way: 'For Thou hast made us for Thyself, and our heart can find no rest until it rests in Thee.'[1]

Within each of us lives an empty space, a vacuum that nothing can fill except fellowship with the Father. God created our hearts to yearn for Him, to seek His face. In the quietness of our hearts, we ask, we seek, we knock, and God makes us a promise:

> Ask and it will be given to you; seek and you will find; knock and the door will be opened to you. For everyone who asks receives; he who seeks finds; and to him who knocks the door will be opened (Matt. 7:78).

When we wait for Him, when we watch for Him, when we listen for His voice, we find Him. And through the prayer of the seeking heart, we come to know Him, our Creator, the One who promises us rest.

Jesus and Elijah found Him on a mountaintop.

Mama found Him in a flower garden.

I found Him in an ancient deserted monastery.

Have you found Him yet in your secret place?

God has already come to us. Now He waits for us to come to Him.

How often I need to visit the mountaintop, to sit still and listen for the sound of fresh, cool spring water – Living Water that will refill my empty pitcher and give me the strength I need to face the next difficult day. Even though Kappal, Switzerland, is separated from me by time and distance, I keep a bit of Kappal in my heart and travel there often.

---

1. St. Augustine, *Confessions* (Middlesex, England: Penguin, 1961), p. 21.

Alone With the Father

Hot, thirsty, His feet still aching, Jesus finally finishes his all-day preaching marathon. Late that night, the crowds go home, their sponges full and dripping with the rich living water of God's Word.

'Now,' Jesus says to His disciples. 'Get into the boat and row to the other side of the lake. I'll join you later.'

When the boat is out of sight, Jesus places one weary foot in front of the other and climbs up the side of the mountain.

Have you ever wondered what Jesus did when He reached His secret place of prayer?

Did He sing and dance and raise His hands to heaven?

Did He stretch out on the grass, feel the night's dew settle on His face, and talk out loud to the Father?

Did He sit on the mountain's edge and in awe and wonder gaze at the stars He had created?

Did He lie in the dirt face down and cry and agonize over those with leper's sores or blind eyes or crippled legs that He would not have time to touch and heal?

Did He, perhaps, see the vague image of a cross on some far horizon cast in uncanny light by the night's crescent moon?

We aren't told what He did. We are just told that He went alone into the mountains to pray.

I believe Jesus prayed in all these ways and many more. Perhaps Jesus climbed to the mountain's summit, sat still and silent and simply rested in His Father's arms. So very close to the Father, Jesus needed few words, if any, to communicate. Maybe they just sat there together, Father and Son, enjoying each other's presence in quiet, restful fellowship. A prayer without words. A prayer from the heart.

Jesus leaves the mountain and walks toward the lake to meet His friends. But the night will offer Him no rest. Before morning dawns, Jesus will have walked across the lake, rescued

Peter from drowning, and calmed a mischievous malevolent wind.

> When they had crossed over, they landed at Gennesaret and anchored there. As soon as they got out of the boat, people recognized Jesus. They ran throughout that whole region and carried the sick on mats to wherever they heard He was (Mark 6:53-55).

And once again, Jesus faced the demands of a busy workday, a day that would, no doubt, last much longer than nine to five. But, no doubt, Jesus had new zest to His voice when He opened His mouth to speak. There was new vigor in His step. For He had been to the mountaintop. He had dipped His cup into the mountain stream, and His spirit had been refilled.

I can just hear Him now, as He walked toward the waiting crowds:

> If a man has one hundred sheep, but one of the sheep gets lost, he will leave the other ninety-nine sheep on the hill. He will go to look for the lost lamb ... (Matt. 18:12 NCV).

> Listen! A farmer went out to sow his seed. As he was scattering the seed some fell along the path, and the birds came and ate it up. Some fell on rocky places, where it did not have much soil (Mark 4:3-5).

> Stop worrying! Look at the flowers in the field. See how they grow. They don't work or make clothes for themselves. But I tell you that even Solomon with his riches was not dressed as beautifully as one of these flowers (Matt. 6:28-29 NCV).

Deep Peaceful Rest

The prayer of a seeking heart. I remember going shopping as a little girl one Saturday with my mother and Mama. After a full day of trying on clothes and comparing prices, I was exhausted. When Mom pulled into the last shop's parking lot, I asked if I could stay in the car. Mama offered to stay with me, and in the quietness of the front seat, together we waited.

Mama and I had waited together many times before, but for some unknown reason the next few moments in the car became a memory snapshot I filed alongside some of the life-changing high points of my life.

My eyelids heavy, my limbs limp, I leaned my head on Mama's shoulder. I can still hear her rhythmical breathing. I can still feel the soft wool of her coat against my face. I can still smell the familiar scent of lavender from her morning bath. Never have I been more aware of such deep peaceful rest.

Mom finished her errand and we drove home. The extraordinary once again became the ordinary. But I'll never forget that moment when we sat there together, grandmother and granddaughter, enjoying each other's presence in quiet, restful fellowship. When my weary heart seeks rest, that's the kind of comfort I find with the Father. It's worth the long hike up the mountainside. Because there I come to know more intimately the One who loves me, the One I can totally trust, and the One who has promised never to leave me.

How our hearts seek the comforting shoulder of our loving Father! Yet as we live in the hectic pace of everyday life, in the arena of the ordinary, it's easy to overlook the urgent needs of a yearning heart. Life is filled with endless distractions, distractions that shackle our eyes and ears and hands and minds. The heart begs for equal time, but its gentle voice can often not be heard above the swarming crowds.

This is why, dear friend, you and I need a secret place, a place of solitude, where we can find rest with the Father, where we can wait and watch and listen and prepare our hearts to hear His calming and reassuring voice. For God speaks to us in quiet ways, ways we might miss if we fail to retreat to the mountaintop faithfully. How easy it is to miss the extraordinary while we live in the mundane midst of the everyday ordinary.

Living In the Ordinary

The ordinary in life is like figuring our annual income tax. We don't like to do it, but it has to be done. It's much more exciting to experience the extraordinary.

What is the ordinary?

'Mommy, can I have a cookie before supper?'
'Denise, did you pick up my clean shirts from the cleaners?'
'Mom, I need a costume for tomorrow's school talent show!'
'Hey, lady, how'd ya say this sink got stopped up?!'
'Denise, haven't you finished that project yet?'

The demands of the ordinary drain me quickly, and my thirsty heart needs living water. That's when I hear God's gentle call, a call more urgent than the clamor of the crowd. He beckons me to come, come to the mountaintop, far away from the demanding madding crowd. 'C'mon, Denise,' He calls. 'Let's find a quiet place to be alone and get some rest.'

And without excuse, without guilt, I leave the dirty dishes in the sink, the unbalanced checkbook on my desk, and the family room floor unvacuumed. I begin the long steep climb, step by step, up the mountainside to commune with God.

Perhaps you, too, head often up the mountainside. There's no other place in the world like it. One of my favorite authors, Max Lucado, describes his nightly hike. In the late evening, as his family sleeps and the house is quiet, Max slips away to his secret place and listens for the gentle call.

'The quietness will slow my pulse, the silence will open my ears, and something sacred will happen,' he writes. 'The soft slap of sandaled feet will break the stillness, a pierced hand will extend a quiet invitation, and I will follow.... I leave behind the budgets, bills, and deadlines and walk the narrow trail up the mountain with Him ... my sacred summit – a place of permanence in a world of transition.'[2]

---

2. Max Lucado, *The Applause of Heaven* (Dallas, TX: Word Publishing, 1990), pp. 22-23.

Have you been to the mountaintop lately?

Questions for Group Study

1. In what ways was prayer important to Jesus?

2. What does Jesus' own prayer-retreat example say to us today?

3. How important is it to give ourselves permission to rest in the Lord, to seek Him in the midst of a busy day?

4. Why should our own personal prayer time be the first item on our list of priorities?

5. Describe your most recent personal prayer retreat: was it significant?
   a. Were you able to relax from work and hectic schedules, and simply rest in prayer with the Lord?
   b. Did you feel pangs of guilt for taking time off? If so, how did you deal with those feelings?
   c. When do you plan to take your next prayer retreat? (As a group, share prayer-retreat ideas and places.)

6. What does this statement made by St. Augustine say to you? 'For thou hast made us for Thyself, and our heart can find no rest until it rests in Thee.'
   a. Do you find that statement true in your own life? How?

7. What significant meanings do the image of the mountaintop hold in Scripture? (Look up the following verses and discuss them):
   a. Exodus 3:1-12
   b. Numbers 33:38
   c. Deuteronomy 34:1-8
   d. 1 Kings 18:15-40
   e. Matthew 5–7
   f. Mark 5:11
   g. Luke 6:12

Suggestions for Personal Reflection

- Plan a prayer retreat. Arrange for a few days of uninterrupted solitude and plan to meet the Lord in a special place.

- Choose a place not too far away from your home so that your prayer time will not be used up in long travel.

- If you invite a friend to go with you, discuss before you go how you will schedule your days. Help her to understand the purpose of the retreat and the time you will need to be alone.

- If going away from home, even for a short time, will not work out, plan a mini-retreat. Schedule several hours, or as much time as possible, and find a secret place where you can rest and pray without interruption.

THREE

WAITING FOR THE LORD TO PASS BY

We don't know her name. We know only that she is a Jewish woman with an embarrassing medical problem. For the past twelve long and hurtful years she has bled continuously. She has spent all her money on doctors who promised sure cures for a hemorrhaging problem. But her bleeding continues. Unchanged.

Money spent, energy drained, she is exhausted. Frustrated, sad, lonely, she has almost given up hope. She has stood on the mountaintop for years, praying with a weary heart, and wondering why the God of Abraham has not heard her cries for healing. She looks to her Father for relief, for a single ray of hope, for just one day without the loss of blood, yet she faces silence. Painful silence.

The disease that afflicts her is especially humiliating in her society. The law also prohibits her from touching anyone else, lest they be made unclean. Levitical law requires her to shout, 'Unclean! Unclean!' loud enough so that the town's people can clear a wide path to let her pass. She is a woman with a humiliating illness, and until she meets Jesus, she can find no cure.

A Broken Promise

Her name is Sarah, and, to her deep distress, her menstrual menses has ceased. Years before, her closest friends came to her each month, always asking the same question: 'Sarah? Sarah?'

Sarah already knew what they would ask, and she appreciated their concern. But with each inquiry, her eyes would fill with tears as she sadly shook her head.

'I'm so sorry, Sarah, so sorry. But, Sarah, keep trusting God. Maybe ... maybe next month He will send the child,' they would encourage her.

For years Sarah has waited and hoped and prayed for the child God promised to her and to her husband Abraham. But now her time has passed. Her childbearing years have come to an end. Full of sorrow, she gives the wooden cradle, the tiny handmade gown, and soft lamb's wool blanket to a young expectant friend. 'I will no longer dream of becoming a mother,' she whispers under her breath. 'God hasn't heard my prayer. God did not keep His promise.'

She feels she has disappointed Abraham, that she has failed him as a woman, as a wife. For several years he has seemed more and more withdrawn. She now spends her days slumped to her knees by the kitchen fire, crying in despair for the unborn children that will never be.

Infertility – the curse of the Hebrew woman in Sarah's time. Sarah is embarrassed by her barrenness. Yet, beyond her empty womb lies the most painful awareness of all. The God in whom her heart dwells will not answer her. And her world has become strangely silent. No hungry baby cries for her in the night. Her friends no longer ask her if.... And the One in whom she has placed her trust, her expectation, her life, is silent.

The Promised Messiah

Her name is Eve, and she has just discovered she is with child. Outside the gates of Eden, she gives quiet thanks to God, the One with whom she used to walk and talk.

She sadly recalls the deceiving serpent, her wrong choices, her sin and God's punishment to her and to Adam. They failed God – both of them. They disobeyed their Creator. They are judged guilty. They are banished from the Garden. They have known God's paradise, but now, in their time of despair and endless waiting, they are living and working in paradise lost.

Eve places a calloused hand on her swollen middle and remembers God's warning to her deceiver:

> I will put enmity between you and the woman, and between your seed and her Seed; He shall bruise your head, and you shall bruise His heel' (Gen. 3:15 NKJV).

In intense shame, she didn't understand her Creator's words to the serpent. But now, after a time of repentance and reflection, God's words make perfect sense to her. 'Her Seed.' It would be by the woman that the Savior would come.[1] Redemption, restoration, re-entry into Paradise would come through God's chosen One ... the One who would be born by a woman's seed.

'Yes,' she smiles and looks up to the heavens. She, Eve, the mother of all life, would be the mother of the promised Messiah.

'After this time of God's silence,' she tells her husband, 'God now hears, God now speaks.' And prayers of thanksgiving pour from her heart, a heart cut in two by the knife of rejection.

The pregnancy is difficult. After a long and painful delivery, Eve births a beautiful dark-haired boy and calls him Cain. And for the first time in a long time, she feels a bit of hope stir within her heavy heart. Then Eve gives birth to yet another boy. She names him Abel.

---

1. See Galatians 4:4.

Eve watches her two sons grow and learn and become strong men. She notices how skillfully one tills the ground and the other tends the sheep. She observes with a mother's pride each son as he gives his finest fruit and his flock's first-born to God as an offering. In day-to-day anticipation, she watches closely for God's Messianic promise to be fulfilled. And each morning when she awakes from slumber, she looks toward the guarded gate and dreams a dream of paradise.

But one day, Eve's dream becomes a mother's worst nightmare. Jealousy erupts between brothers: Cain, her firstborn, slays Abel, her second.

And God is silent.

In one tragic afternoon, Eve loses both sons. And Eve loses all hope for freedom from sin's bondage.

Does God Hear You

Are you suffering in pain and confusion, and no matter how long you pray, no matter how long you wait, you think God isn't listening?

Are you sinking into the quicksand of despair, your trust in God beginning to wane, for no matter how hard you pray, God never seems to answer?

Are you beginning to lose hope because your dreams have been dashed, and even though you pray sincerely, God seems far away?

I, too, have felt this way. I have sometimes felt like the man John Bunyan's Christian once met in his journey of faith, the man locked in the iron cage in the very dark room.

'Now, the man, to look on, seemed very sad,' writes Bunyan. 'He sat with his eyes looking down to the ground, his hands folded together, and he sighed as if he would break his heart.'

"Then Christian said to the man, "What art thou?" The man answered, "I am what I was not once.... I was once a fair and flourishing professor ... I was once, as I thought, fair for the

Celestial City, and had even joy at the thoughts that I should get thither.'

"'Well, but what art thou now?' asked Christian.

"'I am now a man of despair, and am shut up in it, as in this iron cage. I cannot get out. Oh, now I cannot!'"[2]

The iron cage of despair. Have you been there? Are you now there, trying hard to wait, trust, and hope, but feeling discouraged and wondering where God is while you hurt?

Verna Birkey writes about St. John of the Cross's 'dark night of the soul' – that state of silent desperation. They are those painful hours, days, months, years, that no matter how hard we pray, God seems silent.

'Nearly all the great saints of the past talk about "the dark night of the soul," she writes, 'when God seemed far removed and answers didn't come.'[3]

Job experienced the dark night of the soul when, within a short span of time, he tragically lost his health, his children, and his wealth. Covered with oozing sores, he cried out in search of God:

Oh, that I knew where I might find Him ... Look, I go forward, but He is not there, and backward, but I cannot perceive Him ... I cannot behold Him; ... I cannot see Him (Job 23:3, 8, 9 NKJV).

David also prayed to God from his 'very dark room':

to You I call, O Lord my Rock; do not turn a deaf ear to me. For, if You remain silent, I will be like those who have gone down to the pit. Hear my cry for mercy as I call to You for help (Ps. 28:1, 2).

Jerusalem destroyed, the Temple burned, the Children of Israel captured as prisoners in Babylon, Jeremiah wailed from his own iron cage:

---

2. John Bunyan, *The Pilgrim's Progress* (Old Tappan, NJ: Fleming H. Revell Co., 1974 [originally published 1688], p. 35.

3. Verna Birkey, *If God Is In Control, Why Is My World Falling Apart?*

> [God] has walled me in so I cannot escape; He has weighed me down with chains. Even when I call out or cry for help, He shuts out my prayer (Lam. 3:7, 8.).

> Why do You always forget us? Why do You forsake us for so long? (Lam. 5:20).

Is this not the question all of us have asked at one time or another?

The great prophet, Elijah, when pursued by the head-hunting, bloodthirsty Queen Jezebel, sank deep into the pit of hopelessness within the bowels of Beersheba's wilderness.

> 'I have had enough, LORD,' Elijah cried. 'Take my life; I am no better than my ancestors' (1 Kings 19:4).

Even Jesus, Himself, dying on a Roman cross called out to His Father in agony and question:

> My God, my God, why have You forsaken me? (Matt. 27:46).

> Far worse than the breaking of [Jesus'] body is the shredding of His heart. His own countrymen clamored for His death. His own disciple planted the kiss of betrayal. His own friends ran for cover. And now His own father is beginning to turn His back on Him, leaving Him alone.[4]

Forsaken. Alone. Sinking rapidly into the realm of resignation. Crying out to God in torment and hearing only the inaudible beat of His own broken heart.

I've been there too. Feeling alone and forsaken by God, I begged the Lord to heal my dying father. I knelt at my dad's bedside for seven months in 1999 waiting to hear God's voice. I experienced the 'dark night of the soul' for many months, and it seemed almost unending. Did God finally answer my prayers? Yes. But not in the way I had asked. Instead of renewed and healed life, God allowed my dad to die. It took several

---

4. Max Lucado, *Six Hours One Friday* (Portland, OR: Multnomah Press, 1989), p. 23.

years before I finally came to terms with God's silence, and God's refusal to heal my father. In fact, I wrote a book about my father, prayer, and my long journey. I titled the volume *Tilling the Soil: Prayer Penetrates Our Pain* (Zondervan, 2005). In the volume, I reach out to others who wait for God's answer and even wonder if God hears their prayers.

Darkness – The Time to Listen

What should you and I do when our weary hearts cry out to God and He doesn't respond? What are we to do when we beg God to answer our prayers and we are met with unexplained silence?

Within God's Word rests the secret. Within the lives of history's most faithful believers lives the answer. If we listen hard enough, we can hear God's gentle oft-spoken whisper: 'Dear daughter, I have a reason for My silence. You are Mine, and because you are Mine, I can trust you with My silence. Wait. Be still ... and know.'

The secret? The answer? The heart's preparation to receive God's silence?

Faithfully waiting ... quietly, prayerfully, attentively waiting ... waiting for the Lord to pass by. Waiting ... waiting with prayer-filled hearts and finely-tuned ears ... waiting, listening, trusting, hoping. Sitting alone in the iron cage in a very dark room ... knowing your Father is beside you and that you are never alone. 'Are you in the dark just now in your circumstances, or in your life with God?' asks Oswald Chambers. 'Then remain quiet ... Darkness is the time to listen.'[5]

When God was silent, Elijah simply, prayerfully, stood on the mountainside and watched, listened, and waited for God to reveal Himself. And God did reveal Himself to Elijah, in His own way, in His own time.

God also revealed Himself to David who, with great patience, endured God's silence: 'I waited patiently for the LORD,' he later

---

5. Oswald Chambers, *My Utmost for His Highest* (New York: Dodd, Mead, and Company, 1935), p. 7.

wrote. 'He turned to me and heard my cry. He lifted me out of the slimy pit ... He set my feet upon a rock' (Ps. 40:1-3.)

Far from home, and made to wait in Babylonian chains, Jeremiah could one day shout with joy:

> The LORD is good to those whose hope is in Him, to the one who seeks Him; it is good to wait quietly for the salvation of the LORD (Lam. 3:25-26, my emphasis).

After my father died at Christmastime, and my emotions were torn, bruised, and confused, I could not say with Jeremiah 'the Lord is good ....' Christmas cards expressing holiday joy, and sympathy cards renewing my grief, both filled my home's mailbox. It would take several years before I could know with absolute assurance that 'the Lord is good....' And He is! So very good!

It takes great faith to wait quietly, patiently, for the Lord. It takes great trust to know that God has a purpose in our waiting. And while we wait, we can be certain that God does hear the quiet prayers of our hearts. 'Call upon Me and come and pray to Me, and I will listen to you,' He promises. 'You will seek Me and find Me, when you seek Me with all your heart!' (Jer. 29:12-13).

An attentive heart, a prayerful heart, is a searching heart. And the closer our hearts to God, the softer He needs speak to them. In the stillness of what seems to us a bottomless void, we can know that God hears.

> A wonderful thing about God's silence is that the contagion of His stillness gets into you and you become perfectly confident – 'I know God has heard me.' His silence is the proof that He has.[6]

God has planted in our hearts the faith to know, and even when our minds cannot understand Him, cannot comprehend Him, our hearts urge us to trust, to hope, to move onward through the fog of faith.

---

6. Chambers, *My Utmost for His Highest*, p. 285.

'Faith begins when I can no longer see, no longer understand.... I need the grace of endurance to forge ahead through the blackness. When I can see the outcome, that isn't faith.[7] So, we press forward steadily through the dark nights of our souls until God breaks the consuming silence and we hear His reassuring voice. And in God's seemingly timeless hush, while we seek Him with all our hearts, He reveals Himself in ways unexpected, in ways pregnant with surprising promise.

> You will find that God has trusted you in the most intimate way possible, with an absolute silence, ... because He saw that you could stand a bigger revelation.[8]

God trusted me with His silence during those long days by my dad's bedside. I sought Him with all my heart. I searched the Scriptures to affirm His promises. For almost one year during my dad's illness, I thought about little else but prayer. I yearned to hear God speak to my heart and give me comfort, reassurance, and understanding. But God had different plans. With His unmistakable silence, He forced me to a greater understanding. He made me search my heart and His Word for comfort and reassurance. And, in the end, He gave me a revelation about Himself and prayer that changed my life and the way I pray.

The Lord Passes By

So, dear woman, whose hemorrhaging never ceases. Continue to wait, you who, for twelve years, are shunned by the religious society of your day, you who knows the disgrace of a disease that deems you socially unclean. Listen to your ancestor, David, when he tells you to 'rest in the LORD and wait patiently for Him' (Ps. 37:7). Wait, for in a short time, the Lord will pass by.

And when the Lord passes by you, don't be shy. Weave your way through the crowds, reach out and touch His robe, and let

---

7. Birkey, *If God Is In Control, Why Is My World Falling Apart?*, p. 93.
8. Chambers, *My Utmost for His Highest*, p. 285.

your long-suffering faith in God bring you healing. For the Lord will reward your faith in Him, and your healing will bring glory to the Father – in your own day and in a day 2000 years in the future.

Then go ... go and let the righteous rabbis examine you. Be full of joy when they loudly pronounce you 'clean' again! Dance through the marketplace laughing, touching those you love, and patting village youngsters' heads. Dream your dreams for a husband and children. And spend the rest of your life praising the One who hears and answers prayer, and reveling in your newfound revelation.

And you, Sarah, remain in God even though your child-bearing years are past. Even though you are living in the pit of despair, continue to trust Him, Sarah, even in your barrenness. For God is a God of miracles.

> [God] waits for us to despair of human strength and then intervenes with heavenly. God waits for us to give up and then – surprise![9]

Watch for His divine intervention, Sarah. And while you wait in prayer, you might want to retrieve the cradle, gown, and baby blanket? Stop crying; start knitting! You don't know it now, but God has a delightful surprise, nay, shock, nay, bombshell! in store for you and Abraham. And 2 millenniums later, people will still be talking about it!

Wait a few more years, until the eve of your second century of life. Then look to the stars and imagine their number. Run your fingers through the sea's sand and count the grains. For your unborn children of many generations will out-number both.

And brace yourself, Sarah, for an angelic visitor. Be careful not to laugh when you receive the unbelievable news. If you

---

9. Lucado, *Six Hours One Friday*, p. 161.

must laugh, chuckle from joy, not from disbelief. For you, Sarah, will become a mother. A new mother! An old new mother!

When baby Isaac arrives, trumpet your announcements, doll him up, and show him to your friends. For his birth will show a nation, nay, a world, that God does, indeed, keep His promises.

I've a message for you, too, Eve. Never give up hope. For even in His silence, God is a God of hope. God hears your prayers even as you pray outside the gates of Eden.

No, Eve, you will not be the mother who bears the promised Messiah. This is not in God's perfect plan. But one day, one day in God's time, a Jewish woman will birth the Savior. He will come just as God has promised. And through the seed of a woman, the seed of your daughter's daughter's daughter's daughter, He will redeem a fallen race. He will come to free all humankind from sin's bondage. And He will be called the Second Adam. With His own life, He will bring reconciliation to a prodigal world and reopen the gates of paradise.

Questions for Group Study

1. If you feel led to do so, ponder these questions as a group:

   a. 'Are you suffering in pain and confusion, and no matter how long you pray, no matter how long you wait, you think God isn't listening?'

   b. 'Are you sinking quickly into the quicksand of despair, your trust in God beginning to wane, and no matter how hard you pray, God never seems to answer?'

   c. 'Are you beginning to lose hope because your dreams have been dashed, and even though you pray sincerely, God seems far away?'

2. The iron cage of despair – have you ever been there?

a. Have you ever been trapped in a hard situation and thought there was no way out? What did you do? How did you progress through it?

b. Was waiting in prayer, continuing in prayer, helpful to you?

c. Have you ever felt so discouraged that you wondered where God was while you hurt? Do you feel that way now? If so, please explain.

3. What should you and I do when our weary hearts cry out to God and He doesn't respond? What are we to do when we beg God to answer our prayers and we are met with unexplained silence?

a. How would you counsel a friend who came to you with these perplexing problems in her prayer life?

4. Do you agree that the answer to God's silence is 'faithfully waiting ... quietly, prayerfully, attentively waiting ... waiting for the Lord to pass by. Waiting ... waiting with a prayer-filled heart and finely-tuned ears ... waiting, listening, trusting, hoping'?

a. Why or why not?

b. In what other ways can we deal with God's silence? List in order of importance.

5. 'Call upon Me and come and pray to Me, and I will listen to you,' He promises. 'You will seek Me and find Me, when you seek Me with all your heart.' What does this verse in Jeremiah 29:12-13 mean to you?

6. Have you ever known the silence of God only to discover that He has entrusted to you a bigger revelation? If so, will you describe the situation?

Suggestions for Personal Reflection

If prayer has become difficult for you, here are some suggestions:

· Reread the example of prayer given to us by Jesus, Himself, in Matthew 6:9-13. Repeat the words of the prayer until you once again feel God's closeness and can once again pray the prayer without words.

· Simply rest in prayer. Find a quiet place and listen as the Lord speaks to your heart.

· In your quiet time, read some of your favorite verses of Scripture. Then close your eyes and contemplate the meaning of each. Allow God to speak to you through His Word.

· If you are experiencing your 'dark night of the soul,' seek the advice and help of a Christian counselor, pastor, family member, or friend with whom you can confide and share.

· Attend to the practical matters of life, such as: Are you getting enough sleep? Are you eating regularly and wisely? Do you take time out during your busy days to rest? Are you presently involved in hard situations that you find difficult to deal with? (Often, a better schedule, a less stressful day, and/or a timely visit to a medical doctor for a thorough physical examination can be helpful to your prayer life.)

SECTION II

THE LISTENING HEART

(When we hear His gentle whisper, we come to love God.)

Then a great and powerful wind tore the mountains apart and shattered the rocks before the LORD, but the LORD was not in the wind.

After the wind there was an earthquake, but the LORD was not in the earthquake.

After the earthquake came a fire, but the LORD was not in the fire. And after the fire came a gentle whisper.

(1 Kings 19:11-12)

FOUR

LISTENING FOR THE FATHER'S VOICE

The gentle tap of summer's rain beckons me to stretch my nine-year-old frame upon the family-room floor and listen. I feel an unexpected cool August breeze blow my pig-tailed braids as it passes through the back porch screen door. The woodsy scent of summer drifts through the hickory nut trees, and renews my play-tired body, refreshes my childish spirit. The music played by the symphony of ten thousand raindrops upon the tin porch roof of my grandparents' farmhouse lullabies me into deep rest. Ten, twenty, thirty, forty years will flow by, and much of my childhood will be forgotten. But the spectacular tap-tap-tap upon the tin roof will always induce in me a sense of childhood remembrance and restful serenity.

'Nisey?' Mama calls softly and lightly strokes my tousled hair. 'Nisey? Wake up, Nisey.'

I stretch long and lazy like an old calico cat, and then spring swiftly to my feet. It's that time of day, the hour I most await. Lunch! Mama's magnificent lunches!

Crispy fried children, Papa's Big Boy tomatoes, hot buttered corn straight from the garden and still on the cob! I can already smell cornbread baking, fresh okra frying in the black cast iron skillet, and pound cake – rich and sweet – cooling on the wooden counter.

Mama's traditional southern lunch. I would hold onto the aroma that overflowed my grandmother's small kitchen long after the okra and tomatoes and corn ceased to grow in the backyard sunshine.

Lunch is over. My tummy is filled. The rain has stopped. Summer's sun has resurfaced. I am renewed. And, in no time, I am splashing through the puddles and running beneath the branches of the backyard shade trees, unaware that the happy days of childhood upon that little farm won't last forever.

Childhood. How beautiful it can be. How quickly it passes by. How short the season of spring and summer within the span of one's existence. For with the end of summer comes suitcases stuffed with memories and the long trip toward the advent of autumn.

I'll never forget the year I turned forty. It crept up on me like a tiger, then pounced and took me by surprise. I wasn't ready for it.

On my 40th birthday, so longing for the disappearing little girl in me to tarry, I bought myself a pair of roller skates – hot pink roller skates. My friends laughed. They knew I hadn't skated in thirty years. But I skated anyway. For a little while. Then I went home, soaked my aching muscles and skinned knees in a tub of hot water, and took a nap. A long nap!

When I turned 50, and hit the half-century mark, I was expecting the shock. I did nothing very spectacular. I had long ago put my hot pink roller skates away. Now I am 55! I get a senior's discount on my coffee at most fast food restaurants.

John Patrick in *The Teahouse of the August Moon* says that 'pain makes men think.' I say: 'Fifty-five makes women think!' It took at least six months for me to muster up the courage needed to ask for my senior's coffee discount. When I finally choked out: 'I'll take the senior discount, please,' I was disappointed when they didn't give me a look of disbelief, question my age, or ask for my driver's license for proof. Now it doesn't bother me. It's worth the humiliation to save the dime.

But how different life looks on this side of youth – the side that offers fewer years left than one has yet lived. Recently I saw a photograph of my grandmother in 1951, the year I was born. Gray hair. Rounding figure. Cotton print housedress. It dawned upon me that I am now older than Mama was at my birth. Now she is gone, as is my grandfather, and my father. And the young green tomatoes Papa left on the vines on the morning of his death have long ago ripened blood red and fallen away, never to grow again.

Now, almost a decade and a half later, while the weeds overcome the once-bountiful gardens, I sit by a screen door on an August afternoon and dream of the symphony of a long-ago rain.

The Death of a Childhood

Have you ever paused and wondered: What is the use of life? The moment we are born, we begin to die. We live, we work, we hurt, we lose, we love ... and we die. What is the use of life?

I feel drawn to deeper contemplation of this century-un-changing question when I most keenly feel the heartbroken-ness of loss. Or when I feel the sadness of the years that frus-trate my desire to spring to my feet with the nimbleness of a nine-year-old. Or when I miss those with whom I shared a piece of my heart, those whose most inward thoughts became my thoughts, those whose words and kindnesses I carry in the treasure chest of my soul.

Perhaps I ponder it most passionately when I realize how much, even now, I miss Mama and Papa, and the warm summer rain and the unexpected cool August breeze and the fresh okra frying in the cast iron skillet. For when they passed on, a part of me passed on with them. In some ways, Mama's and Papa's passing signaled the passing of my childhood.

And nobody calls me 'Nisey' any more.

Not long ago, at her request, I had lunch with a 'forty-something-year-old' Christian woman I had not met before. She just wanted to talk, for she had a heart full of frustration.

As she began to pour out her story, I thought of the many other women who had recently relayed the same message to me. Basically, she was tired. The load of teen-rearing and housework and full-time job had taken its toll on her body, mind, and spirit. Her job outside the home held little meaning, offered few dollars, and discouraged her God-given creative talents. Spiritually, by her own admission, she was empty, stale, depleted. She didn't hear the Father's voice anymore.

'The child in me enjoyed the parade of life, the surprises, the noises, the festive floats that flew so quickly by,' she cried. 'The adult that I am, however, sees the parade of life in a different light. It brings some joy, but the surprises hold no wonderment any more. The noise is often too loud and confusing, and the festivity is over before I am ever able to make much sense of it. While I try to contemplate the deeper meaning of the parade, a profusion of pandemonium passes by.'

Her parade metaphor pictured precisely her problem. With every painful sentence, I heard the same unspoken plea:

What's the use of life? Of work? Of prayer? What is really important in this ongoing parade of life, a parade that will proceed with or without my presence?

Just what do you tell someone who is frustrated with life, finds prayer difficult, and no longer feels God's presence? What can she do – what can you and I do – when we hit a stalemate in our faith? How can we tune in and once again prepare our hearts to listen and hear the Father's voice?

Dust Bowl Faith

Flat faith. I've been there, there in the pit of despair, so depressed, so discouraged, so far from feeling my Father's nearness. The faith that has lost its sparkle, its vitality, its expectation is not an uncommon encounter for women today.

Perhaps you are there now. Or perhaps you've been there in the past.

Faith residing in the great Dust Bowl. Perhaps you remember the Dust Bowl, or you've heard your parents or grandparents talk about it. More than 50 million green growing acres in the Great Plains region of the southwestern United States turned to dust in the 1930s.

Why? Insufficient rain was one reason. But the primary cause was misuse and neglect of the soil. Before and during World War I, farmers dug up natural vegetation that protected the soil, and planted large crops of wheat. With the wheat and the money rolling in, they didn't consider the needs of the unsecured soil. The grown wheat couldn't protect the land during the frequent hot, dry periods. Eventually, after years of disregard, the rich dark earth turned to dust, and severe wind storms swept the earth right out from under the farmers' feet.

Neglected prayer time, disregarded Bible study, and lack of regular and meditative fellowship with the Father lead to a personal dust bowl of faith. But there is hope. In Christ, there is always hope.

You tell me you no longer hear God's whisper? You no longer feel His presence? You want to find faith's Fountain of Youth and dip yourself into its cool spring water and be bathed with spiritual renewal? You want to wash off the dust of discouragement and once again feel the living, breathing flesh of faith?

Come. Take my hand. Let us journey through the dust bowl together.

Appointment with the Lord

First stop. You and I sit on a hillside covered with tender young pines. Except for the sound of a soft breeze, all is quiet. The world sleeps. We watch as the sky turns from midnight blue to rose to the golden shade of sunrise. The stars that peeked out through the dark blanket of sky only minutes before, disappear. We can see just a sketchy trace of a half moon. We do not speak; we listen, we listen to the sounds of silence. We sit still on the grassy hillside in the presence of God, the Creator of light and sunrises and moon and stars ... and we delight in His goodness and generosity.

When we sit quietly with the Lord, waiting, watching, listening, we sit in the presence of a Friend. We need no words. For within us our hearts spill over with gratitude, with child-like wonderment.

In the quiet, you turn to me with a question. 'How,' you ask, 'how can anyone sit on an early morning hillside and see the beauty of the waking universe and not believe in God?'

I don't have an answer. I, too, sit and wonder: 'Oh Lord, for this lovely universe, for this magnificent morning sunrise, to whom does the nonbeliever say, "thank you"?'

Morning is the time for prayerful listening. Every morning, on appointment with the Lord, in a secret place.

Jesus loved the mornings.

> Early the next morning, Jesus woke and left the house while it was still dark. He went to a place to be alone and pray (Mark 1:35 NCV).

After the death of her baby granddaughter, her namesake, and on the road to spiritual renewal, Catherine Marshall awaited each morning's sunrise.

'I am beginning to look forward to these early morning times,' she writes. 'There is an air of expectancy inside me as I watch the sun rise and wait for the Lord.'[1]

She continues: 'I'm beginning to understand why it is so important that I begin my recovery period early in the morning.... In the early morning we are freshest in body, mind, and spirit. There is the freshness of the day itself. It is quiet. Fewer distractions and voices to jam the wave-lengths between us and the Lord.[2]

I, too, love the mornings. I especially enjoy those quiet times, still snuggled under nighttime blankets, my mind hanging somewhere in the land between sleep and fully-alert, when I hear God's voice so plainly. He speaks to my waking heart, and without mental distraction, my heart 'hears' Him.

Meeting the Lord in the early mornings means starting our day in a wonderful way, and keeping the rich close fellowship with Him alive all during the day. Author Warren Wiersbe explains:

I cannot emphasize too much the importance of daily quiet time with the Lord.... Meeting God in the morning means that you fellowship with Him all day long. At different times during the day, you will find the Holy Spirit speaking to you. Listen! There will be occasions when your heart will reach out for God. Pause and love Him! It is as you abide in Him all day long that He is able to work in and through you.[3]

So, friend, let us climb that grassy hillside, sit in our secret place early every morning, and meet the Lord there. Let us bask in the sunrise of His love for us, and thank Him for the privilege of His presence. For 'the life of God given to [people] is the same life that energizes the entire cosmos. It sustains the universe. It is the essence of being. The best a mere mortal can do is to go

---

1. Catherine Marshall, *Light in My Darkest Night* (Old Tappan, NJ: Chosen Books, 1989), p. 211.

2. *Ibid.*, p. 231.

3. Warren W. Wiersbe, *Five Secrets of Living* (Wheaton, IL: Living Books, 1977), p. 83.

quietly to some place, still, alone, there to meditate before the splendor of our God.'[4]

Thanking God in the Waiting Moments

Second stop. You and I climb into my little tan Camry and we take off. Traffic jams. Long red lights. Backed up tunnels. Stalled cars. Halting cars. (And we thank God for the few moments He gives us in our waiting to think about Him.)

In and out of the car all day. Buy skim milk at the grocery store. Pick up stamps at the post office. Fill our tank with expensive gasoline at the station. Deposit a check at the bank. Wait in line at the dry cleaners.

Long lines. Everywhere. Waiting, advancing forward one step, moving back two steps. Just the average day of today's busy woman, wife, mother, grandmother.

(And we thank God for the few moments He gives us in our waiting to think about Him.)

For the Christian, long lines and stalled cars in the fast flow of life's traffic invite opportunities to meditate. In those precious minutes, we center our thoughts on God, and we wonder, we ponder, we remember, and our hearts take on the challenge of understanding God's grace. Constant communion with the Father keeps our spirits renewed, our faith refreshed. For God is only a thought away, a prayer away. Always. When God is in our hearts, He's never very far from our minds. We call it 'Christian meditation.'

What is Christian meditation?

Meditation is the activity of calling to mind, contemplating, thinking over, dwelling on, and applying to oneself, the various concepts that one knows about the promises, purposes, and ways of God.[5]

---

4. Phillip Keller, *A Shepherd Looks at The Good Shepherd and His Sheep* (Grand Rapids, MI: Zondervan Publishing House, 1978), p. 108.

5. Ray Burwick, *Self-Esteem: You're Better Than You Think* (Wheaton, IL: Tyndale House Publishers, Inc., 1983), p. 79.

Christian meditation is a form of silent prayer, the prayer of the heart. While our bodies know the bondage of grocery store lines and traffic-jammed cars, our minds and hearts are free, free to roam unhindered throughout the heavens. Free to enjoy the presence of God. And, because of grace, God's amazing, unlimited grace, our minds and hearts can speak – uninhibited – to the Creator of the heavens.

While some see prayer as simply a religious exercise, you and I can know that prayer is 'the very breath and heartbeat of our lives.' Prayer is 'a friend sharing his heart with his Friend and growing in love and faith.'[6]

Listening to the Lord Through Scripture

Third stop. Sit here silently with me and let us open God's Word. Scripture is the primary way we listen to the Father's voice. It is yet another way to pray.

[God] speaks to us in His Word, and we speak to Him from our hearts.[7]

As you and I sit silently together and read the Scriptures, we hear an unusual shuffle of feet beside us.

'Denise?' you whisper. 'Listen!'

Instinctively, at the same time, you and I turn around to look.

'Useless! Useless! Completely useless!' blurts out the stranger in royal blue garb. 'All things are useless. What do people really gain from all the hard work they do here on earth? People live, and people die. But the earth continues forever.'

The strange old man looks you and me directly in the eye. We are too stunned to speak.

Everything is boring.... Words come again and again to our ears. But we never can hear enough.... There is nothing new here on earth (Eccles. 1:1-4, 8, 9 NCV).

---

6. Wiersbe, p. 42.
7. *Ibid.*, p. 42.

'Solomon?!' You punch my arm and we both stare with mouths agape.

What an opportunity! We fire questions at Solomon point blank as he pauses and considers his response to each inquiry. Then, across the miles of unmarked millenniums, he speaks his words of wisdom. You and I listen. Spellbound.

> 'Are you two living for the Lord or for the things of the world?' he sets his thick dark brow and asks us. 'Remember, I knew God and was greatly blessed by Him, yet I turned from the Lord and went my own way. No wonder I became pessimistic and skeptical as I looked at life! I didn't have God's perspective because I wasn't living for God's purposes.... Turn from the futility of sin and the world, and put your faith in Jesus Christ.'[8]

Before we can catch our breath, we hear another voice.

> 'Do not love the world or the things in the world, you two,' the voice forcefully interrupts. 'If anyone loves the world, the love of the Father is not in him. These are the evil things in the world: wanting things to please our sinful selves, wanting the sinful things we see, being too proud of the things we have....'

You punch me again and point. 'John?!' you ask. We are wide-eyed.

> 'None of those things comes from the Father,' John continues. 'All of them come from the world. The world is passing away. And everything that people want in the world is passing away. But the person who does what God wants lives forever' (1 John 2:15-17 NCV).

Solomon shouts out in hearty agreement.

> 'Life is filled with difficulties and perplexities and there's much that nobody can understand, let alone control. From the human point of view, it's all vanity and folly.'

---

8. Warren W. Wiersbe, *Be Satisfied* (Wheaton, IL: Victor Books, 1990), p. 21. (Paraphrased)

Then, for the first time, we see Solomon smile.

> But life is God's gift to us and He wants us to enjoy it and use it for His glory.[9]

Suddenly, in front of us, One steps forward and holds out His hands, One I have personally known since my ninth year:

> 'Dear children,' He whispers. 'I came to give life – life in all its fullness' (John 10:10 NCV).

The room is expectantly quiet. You and I hold the book tenderly in our hands, the book that has answered life's most perplexing, most quizzical questions, for so many who asked, for so many many years.

In our quiet moment of reading the Scriptures, you and I join hands with Christians across the world, across the centuries. We read the same words of encouragement, the same messages of hope. We read God's Word as if the writers stand beside us, so close to us we hear their breathing, so near we feel their hands resting gently on ours. They share with us their dreams, their visions, their struggles, their revelations, their sorrows, their faith, their lives. And thousands of years later, through their Spirit-inspired words, they come alive to us again and again, and they offer us their most intimate, inward words of hope and love and promise.

'The Bible is God's message to everybody,' writes Elisabeth Elliot. 'We deceive ourselves if we claim to want to hear His voice but neglect the primary channel through which it comes. We must read His Word.... We must live it, which means rereading it throughout our lives.'[10]

We read. And we listen. We listen to the voices that are only quieted when we refuse to hear. You and I hold within our hands, our hearts, living words ... words that speak to us

---

9. Wiersbe, *Be Satisfied*, Foreword.

10. Elisabeth Elliot, *Trusting God in a Twisted World* (Old Tappan, NJ: Fleming H. Revell Co., 1989), p. 127.

from the depths of mystery. Words that open blinded eyes to truth. Words that change lives. Words that offer life ... now and beyond ... life abundant and eternal. Life, given to us as a free gift, but a gift costly to the generous Giver.

Each time you and I open its cover, we step into the pages and meet people of the past like ourselves, people who believe but are often weak, people who trust but sometimes worry, people who follow but unfortunately fall. We find ourselves on every page in those who hurt and question and criticize, in those who drift in and out of the Father's fold, the Father's will.

> As we better understand what the Bible record says, we can better apply it to the needs of people today. This is the work of the imagination – building a bridge of truth from an ancient book to needy hearts today.[11]

'Listen!' you lean over and tell me. 'Do you hear them?'

I listen and I hear the music of a shepherd boy's harp in a far away field as he cares for his sheep and sings a child's praises to God.

I listen and I hear the words of shame and embarrassment pouring from the heart of a woman at a well at noonday as she offers a drink of well water to a tired stranger.

I listen and I hear the sigh of contentment in Daniel's snore as he sleeps in an iron cage next to a ravenous lion that has been divinely reduced to a purring kitty.

I listen and I hear the stuttering Moses speaking to God before a burning bush.

I listen and I hear the rat squeaks in a dungeon, a very dark room that reeks with the stench of dampness, of death, and I watch a chained apostle named Paul scratch on parchment his love for a young church.

---

11. Warren W. Wiersbe, *In Praise of Plodders!* (Grand Rapids, MI: Kregel Publications, 1991), p. 77.

I listen. And I hear the words of mystery, the words of life and death, the words of life everlasting, the secrets of the universe.

> Words and deeds of Christ our Master,
> Pointing to the life and way,
> Still appealing, still inspiring,
> 'Mid the struggles of today.[12]

Calling to the Child Within Us

But before we part, we open the book to one last word, and as we listen, we hear His tender call, His call that beckons us back to childhood. For God calls, not to the hardened and weary adult within us, but to the tender child.

'Come,' He whispers. 'Come to Me as a little child, watching with wonderment, waiting with expectation, listening with anticipation, following with innocence, trusting with sincerity, praying with unceasing simplicity.'

He calls to the little child within us, the child who marvels at the colors of the sunrise; the child who sees Solomon and David and Jesus come alive through Scripture; the child who yearns to strap on hot pink roller skates and take off.

When we listen to the Father's voice, we can hear Him calling back to life the child within you and me. The little girl isn't dead, she just sleeps. And just as Jesus 'woke up' and raised the young daughter of Jairus, He can awaken the child within you and me to life again.

'God grant we may have the wonder of the child-heart that the Holy Spirit gives, and that He may keep our minds young and vigorous and unstagnant, never asleep, but always awake with child-eyed wonder at the next wonderful thing God will do.'[13] I hear my Father's call, and years of adult-encrusted callus

---

12. Ferdinand W. Blanvchard, 'Word of God, Across the Ages,' *The Baptist Hymnal* (Nashville, TN: Convention Press, 1975 edition), p. 148.
13. Chambers, *If You Will Ask*, p. 39.

breaks loose from my heart. I am called back to my Father's simple, serene world of childhood. Free from worry, free from anxiety, free from guilt's bondage, free from the meaningless parade of pandemonium. I am given purpose.

And a life that was tired, frustrated, and spiritually depleted once again splashes in the puddles after an August rain and runs beneath the branches of the backyard's shade trees.

With the voice of the Shepherd, and with the voices of the saints still speaking to my heart, I stretch long and lazy like an old cat. Morning ... the time of day when my 55-year-old body claims yet another day of life, of age. Morning ... the time of day when, through divine mystery, my childlike spirit is refreshed, renewed by a loving Father.

On this new morning, I listen to the gentle tap of summer's rain as it beckons me to rise. A golden-edge sun strains to peek over the horizon, as I lie in bed, snuggled between soft sheets, awaiting my daily awakening.

That's when I hear it, the familiar voice of the One I love, the One who calls me back to the freedom of childhood; the One who calls me to a life lived with purpose; the Shepherd who gave His life for this, His sleeping stretching lamb.

Ever so gently I feel Him stroke my tousled hair, and I hear Him whisper to my listening heart: "Nisey? Nisey? Wake up, Nisey."

Questions for Group Study

1. Ponder your childhood.

    a. Did you enjoy or regret your childhood? Are your memories good or bad?

    b. Did you receive genuine love from your primary caretakers?

    c. Did you receive spiritual nurture?

    d. Do you miss the years of your childhood, and, if so, why?

   e. What events in your childhood proved to be the most significant and why?

2. Have you ever paused and wondered: What is the use of life?

   a. Do you think this is a question asked frequently these days? If so, explain why.

3. Do you have a friend, family member, or acquaintance that is weary of life?

   a. What do you tell someone who is frustrated with life, finds prayer difficult, and no longer feels God's presence?

   b. How can you help this person through her spiritually-dry dilemma?

4. Discuss this statement: 'Neglected prayer time, disregarded Bible study, and lack of regular and meditative fellowship with the Father leads to a personal dust bowl of faith.' Why is this statement true?

5. Do you have a regular time each day to fellowship with the Father? If so, what time of day works best for you and why? Where do you meet the Lord daily? Do you have a particular place? If so, please describe it.

6. Throughout your busy days, do you frequently practice Christian meditation?

   a. What does Christian meditation mean to you?

   b. How has Christian meditation been helpful to keep your mind and heart prepared to pray?

7. Why is the daily reading of, and reflection on, the Word of God essential to our lives as Christians? What does the Bible mean to you personally?

8. Reread the following Scripture passages that deal with the importance of God's Word. What are their meanings: Psalm 19:7-8, 119:105, 130; 2 Timothy 3:16-17; and Hebrews 4:12?

9. How can we 'build a bridge of truth from an ancient Book to needy hearts today?' Is it possible?

Suggestions for Personal Reflection

- Set aside a special time each day to read a portion of Scripture, a time when you are at your freshest and best.

- As you read, pause and ponder over those verses or words you don't fully understand.

- Make notes of all that you want to study more fully.

- Invest in a good Bible dictionary, and keep it close during your devotional times.

FIVE

EARTHQUAKE, WIND, AND FIRE

In need of solitude and silence, and so wanting to be refreshed by uninterrupted communion with the God of creation, I retreat to the sea, the universal setting of serenity.

The rest I find at the shores of the sea has been a rare but refreshing step in my journey of life and faith, as 'the waters turn the soul into a citadel of contented serenity with the spirit ensconced in quiet rest.'[1]

I walk the ocean's edge and spread wide my arms toward its shore, waiting to receive a generous dose of divine rejuvenation. The child within bids me to kick off my shoes and run barefoot through the shell-strewn warm sand. From my pocket I pull a small loaf of bread, and within seconds, I hear the familiar flap of swift wings as seagulls encircle me, shrieking and swooping with silver wings to catch a crumb of crust. The sound of the sea surrounding me, the smell of salt air saturating my lungs, the treasure chest of blue water unfolding before me, my heart is drawn to prayer.

1. W. Phillip Keller, *Sea Edge* (Waco, TX: Word Publishing, 1985), p. 99.

The hush of sea edge. Like a Beethoven sonata, the sea has a language of its own, a common tongue that touches those tired hearts that so seek the simplicity of solitude.

I close my eyes and listen to the gentle waves as they roll upon the shore. I feel an ocean breeze brush my hair, and sea mist kiss my cheek. I wait silently for the familiar sense of serenity to envelope me and whisk from my mind the hard work, hectic schedules, and everyday demands I journey to escape. I push far away from my thoughts the world's people and their problems, as I seek the sea's undisturbed tranquility and peace.

Solitude and Struggle

But, to my dismay and disappointment, this day the sea offers no peace of mind and soul. I find no rest as I pause in seaside presence.

For God has other plans.

I seek solitude, but I am met with struggle. Powerful, prayerful struggle. I yearn to pray the prayer of the waiting heart, the prayer in which I find such gentle peace. Yet I am compelled to pray the prayer of the struggling heart, the prayer of groans and sighs, the prayer of disturbing wordless passion for the world's lost and hurting.

The once welcoming sights and sounds of the sea instead become tsunami-force reminders of a society that wrestles with weariness. The solitude with which I sought to massage my tired muscles, to uplift my listless heart, to renew my sagging soul, now opens the door to the faces, the cries, the perplexity of a planet's people. The sea's restful waters become instead restless waves. Instead of bringing consolation, solitude slaps my face like the salty sea spray. It demands that I open my eyes, my heart, my mind, and take detailed notice of a world that wrenches in pain.

I watch, I wait, I listen, and I am filled with anguish.

I hear the seagull's call, and it sounds like the voice of a small child who cries out in hunger and pain....

I see a lone man walking the distant shore, and I ache with the grief of all those unknown to me who walk alone and are lonely....

I watch a mother and child stand silently by, as waves wash away their dream castle built on sand, and I hear the cries of the newly abandoned and the fatherless child....

I stumble upon the lost limb of a starfish, and I sorrow for those who live with broken dreams and severed spirits, those I will never meet and comfort....

And the solitude I seek far away from the clamor of the crowd becomes the solitude that brings me, oh, so close to them – compassionately close to the world's unknown others. I suffer with those people I will never meet, those strangers I cannot call by name in prayer.

And I learn compassion – the prayer of the heart, the heart of the prayer – the root, stem, and bloom of ministry through Christ to the world's others.

> Thus in and through solitude we do not move away from people. On the contrary, we move closer to them through compassionate ministry.[2]

I want to leave the ocean's edge, those dark turbulent waters that hold the vivid mental images of swollen bellies, pale faces, tear-stained cheeks, twisted limbs, and crushed hearts of a broken humanity. The massiveness of the sea makes me feel so small, so insignificant. I am reduced to one wee voice crying out to God for a fast-sinking society. The perpetual profusion of water holds within its immensity the breadth of our planet's perplexing problems. And I come to understand how weak I am in light of the work that needs so desperately to be done.

My hands reach out toward the sea, and, inside, I crave to hold the world's orphaned children, to build houses for society's

---

2. Henri J. M. Nouwen, *The Way of the Heart* (New York: Ballantine Books, 1981), p. 24.

homeless, to wipe the brows of Earth's battered, to hold the hands of those who have given up hope. But I am weak, so weak, so helpless to alone nurse the wounds of the world. I could more easily hold back the ocean's tide or breathe new life into an abandoned sand dollar than I could alone console Earth's sorrowing society.

I want to run away, far away into the sacred solitude that brings serenity, not suffering. But, alas, I cannot get my heart's consent. For my heart yearns to stay, to wait, to pray. So ... I wait at sea edge. Patiently. I persevere in heartfelt prayer, and I beg God to move me, to convict me, to fill me with His compassion on behalf of a world of others. I pray the prayer of the struggling heart, and deep within I listen ... I listen for the Father's voice in the midst of wind and sea and crashing waves.

Charlotte's Web

I have a new friend who greets me every morning at my bedroom window. I call her Charlotte. All night long she spins and weaves and designs an elaborate web.

I watch with great amazement as she orders her small world, repairs a glistening strand or two, and waits for the dinner bell to ring.

This morning, Charlotte's web speaks to me in a unique way. I cannot carry the spider web analogy too far, however, or it will quickly tear apart. But I have noticed that Charlotte is well aware of what happens within her web. She is sensitive to, and instantly involved in, the least movement on any tender thread of her intricate home. For what happens within Charlotte's webbed world, what touches the lacework of her fragile facility, directly concerns and impacts Charlotte.

I believe the Christian's world is structured less like an orb and more like a web. When, through the prayer of the struggling heart, God grants within us the priceless gift of compassion, we can no longer live with others and stay uninvolved in their lives. We must develop a mission mind. Their hurts, their goals, their dreams become a vital part of our own hearts' prayers. For what happens within our wounded world, what touches the framework of our fragile habitat, directly concerns and impacts the believer in Christ.

Christ's compassion gives us new sensitivity. It commands, equips, and enables us to respond to others in His love, in His power. Through Him, we are challenged, we are empowered to reach out to a hurting world.

If only ... if only we will listen for the Father's voice as he beckons us to prayer.

Prayer of the Struggling Heart

The prayer of the struggling heart. *Does this prayer of our heart, this prayer too deep for words, touch the heart of God?*

During His life on earth, Jesus showed us the Father's heart. For just as Jesus spread His arms and cried over spiritually-blind Jerusalem, I believe God cries over a lost humanity. Scripture affirms that God loves us, His human creation. Christ's weeping heart is but God's heart, a heart made not of stone but of life, living breathing life. If my selfish little heart can be so moved with sympathy for the world's suffering, how much more do His distressed children touch and move the Father's tender heart.

Do our persistent prayers ever change the heart and mind of God? Consider:

> Elijah prayed to God seven times before he saw a small cloud rise up over the sea, a cloud that would replenish the rivers with fresh water and end the deadly drought.[3]

> Abraham prayed to God with nagging, annoying persistence on behalf of the people of Sodom and Gomorrah.

> 'Lord, what if I can find fifty good people? Will You still destroy the city?'

---

3. 1 Kings 18:41-46.

'Abraham, if I find fifty good people in the city of Sodom, I will save the whole city because of them.'

'Well, Lord, what about forty-five?'

'Okay, Abraham, if I find forty-five good people I will not destroy the city.'

'What about forty, Lord?'

'Okay, Abraham, forty.'

'Thirty?'

'Okay, Abraham, thirty.'

And on went the tete-a-tete between Abraham and God until finally ....

'What about ten good people, Lord?'

'You got it, Abraham! If I find ten good people there, I will not destroy the city!'[4]

When we pray, Jesus tells us to ask, to seek, to persist in prayer.

Ask ...; seek ...; knock and the door will be opened to you (Luke 11:9).

Does God respond to our prayers of struggle and sometimes choose to intervene?

Scripture answers this question. Consider:

Jesus touched blind eyes and made them see. He healed lame legs and made them walk. He called friend Lazarus from a grave, and gave him life. The New Testament examples of God's intervention are too numerous to name.

And the Old Testament? Consider:

God parted the great Red Sea and led Moses to save His chosen children. He sheltered a drowning Jonah within a fish's bowel. He used a boy and a slingshot to slay a Philistine giant.

'Yes, Denise,' you say, 'But that's in the Bible. Does God intervene these days when a believer prays?'

---

4. Genesis 18:23-33.

Please allow me to answer with a personal story.

We had been ministering in Boston's inner city, Chelsea, only a few years when street kids set fire to a large tire factory there.

It was an unusually windy day, and firefighters were unable to control the spreading flames. Like the October, 2006, fires in California that killed five firemen, without warning, the blaze changed direction, turned back upon them, and consumed their city fire trucks. Volunteers scrambled to evacuate small children and the elderly from burning apartments. From our upstairs bedroom window, we watched the flames leap from house to house, until they reached the lawn of our home, and their sparks shot hot and loud at our window panes. I phoned my parents in Tennessee as we hurried to pack a few precious photos, an outfit of clothes, and an armful of treasured books and other items.

Mom and Dad were leaving for their church's Wednesday night prayer service.

'Daddy,' I called into the telephone. 'The city is on fire. Our street is next to be evacuated. We're okay and will be leaving the city in a few minutes. So don't worry when you hear the television news reports and can't reach us by phone.'

Then the phone lines went dead.

Several minutes later, I looked at the clock. Eight-thirty. Just as we closed the front door behind us, to the whole city's surprise, the wind suddenly changed direction and died down completely. Weary firefighters fought the remaining flames and quickly forced them under control. Two-thirds of the city was saved from the devastation of fire. Fortunately, the fire claimed neither our home – the parsonage – nor the old rock church.

The next morning, Chelsea awoke to gray skies and air thick with ash. One-third of the city had burned to the ground. Fortunately, no one perished in the flames, and injuries were few. But I can still remember the eerie stillness, the people's shocked faces, and the muffled cries of the city's new homeless.

Two days later, telephone lines were reconnected, and I called my mother. (These were the days – in the early 1970s – before we had cell phones. We were still 'leashed' to land lines!) I told Mom the whole story, the terror I had felt, the closeness of the flames to our home, the people crying in the streets, the city's shelters filling with families. I told her how the wind had suddenly changed direction, and how it had so unexpectedly died down.

'What time did the wind change direction?' she asked.

'Eight-thirty,' I told her.

A long silence separated us. Then she spoke: 'That's the exact time our church prayed for you.'

Hebrews 4:16 tells us to come boldly to the throne of grace, that we may obtain mercy and find grace to help in times of need.

Yes, I believe the living Lord is hard at work today. I believe our prayers do touch His heart. I believe He is able to answer our prayers in whatever way is best to Him.

One thing's for sure. I am convinced that God, through a small church's Wednesday night prayer, changed the course of that Chelsea wind, one thousand miles away, and saved the church and parsonage from the raging fire.

But, it is not important that our prayers might somehow change the mind and heart of God. It is important, however, that we understand how much our prayers greatly change the mind and heart of the one who prays them.

When your heart, when my heart, retreats to a painful solitude and prays the prayer of struggle on behalf of an unknown other, we become different people.

Solitude molds self-righteous people into gentle, caring, forgiving persons who are so deeply convinced of their own great sinfulness and so fully aware of God's even greater mercy that their life itself becomes ministry.[5]

When you and I enter into a dialogue of struggle with the living Lord, we discover anew who we are in this universal web. For when we pray for the brokenness of another, we also pray on behalf of our own brokenness. We, too, know broken hearts – believing hearts filled with Christ's eternal joy, but nonetheless hearts touched by human brokenness. For it is the brokenness of our hearts that lead us to Christ in the first place, the source of our salvation.

How else but through a broken heart may Lord Christ enter in?[6]

How often does the pain of a broken heart drive us to our knees in confession, repentance, and in search of redeeming grace? It is there, in the iron cage of the very dark room of our soul, that we find God's gracious gift of forgiveness. It is there that God whispers to us: 'Child, through my Son, Jesus Christ, I love you, I forgive you, and I give you the gift of life, abundant and forever.'

We are all in the same boat in the immensity of Earth's sea, tossed to and fro by hard-hitting storms, blown off-course and asunder by hard-driving winds. Yet, when we hold out our arms in utter helplessness to the One who can calm the sea, storm, and wind, to the Creator of all the seas, of all the universe, God reaches down and rescues us from the turbulent dark waters. We reach up to Christ in clear understanding of our weakness, our vulnerability, our certain lost-ness, our inability to save ourselves, and we call to Him who will freely extend His arms of grace and pluck us from the tempestuous sea.

Does God save us because in ourselves we are worthy? No. He saves us because He is Love, and Christ's redemption makes us worthy. Salvation is a gift of grace, nothing we can work for,

---

5. Nouwen, p. 22.
6. Attributed to Oscar Wilde.

nothing we can merit, nothing we can ever deserve. Just grace. God-given loving grace.

When we pray with compassion on behalf of others, we enter into the suffering and compassion lived and taught by Christ, Himself. Through the prayer of the struggling heart, we discover anew our unique solidarity within the heart of humankind. As you and I seek solitude, the kind of solitude that solicits struggle, we hear the Father's voice as He calls us to the ministry of loving compassion.

The Prayer of Selfless Struggle

Elijah lived his entire life in loving compassionate ministry to others. He prayed the intense prayer of struggle as he persevered on the mountainside and listened patiently for the Father's voice. Elijah felt deep compassion for the Children of Israel. He grieved to see them live in sin and shortcoming, ignore Yahweh, and bow down and kiss the feet of the false god, Baal.

More than 560 years before the birth of Christ, Elijah waited, Elijah struggled. No doubt, he wanted to turn and run away, but in his time of prayerful solitude, in his time of struggle, his heart would not be moved. He waited, he watched, and he listened. In expectation. In anticipation. He waited with a heart prepared to hear the Father's voice.

When you and I read Elijah's mountainside encounter, can we not somehow sense his dedication to the prayer of the struggling heart? Listen ... can you not hear the turmoil, the fear, the strength of devotion in his voice?

'A great and terrible wind is roaring around me. Great mountain boulders are breaking loose and crashing to the valley below. I am holding on tight in hopes that I, too, won't be blown away by this powerful wind.'

('Elijah,' we tell him: 'Listen to the wind! Listen for the Lord to speak to you. Don't you remember that God once spoke to you in the wind, when the sky became black and clouds rose up over the sea, and rain showered the earth and ended the famine of your prophecy?')

'Yes, I remember it. I am listening in the midst of the wind, but God does not speak. Wait! A great earthquake roars beneath me. The earth shakes and splits around me and threatens to capsize this great mountain. I fear I will be crushed by the earth's violent vibrations.'

('Elijah, continue to listen while the earth quakes round you, for surely God will speak to you above the crash and clamor. He has often spoken to you in dramatic ways, ways steeped in majesty and mystery. Do you not remember the ravens that brought you bread and meat by the Brook Cherith, and the angels who fed you in the Beersheba wilderness? Do you not remember the dead boy God told you to bring back to life? Or the widow's handful of flour that became a bottomless bin? Drama, Elijah, drama and mystery ... watch for God in the sensational, the spectacular.')

'I am listening. I am listening for God to shout to me above the noise and destruction, but God does not speak. God does not speak!

'But, wait.... Fire! Fire engulfs the mountain, the flames sweep around my head and feet. Surely, surely God will speak to me through the fire!'

('Yes, Elijah, God will surely speak to you through the fire, for you have said it yourself: 'God is the God that answers by fire.' Yes, Elijah! Listen, and remember when fire fell from heaven at Mount Carmel and consumed the sacrificed bull, and the wood and stones and dust, and fire even licked up the water from the trench. God spoke through the fire, and the prophets of Baal were destroyed, and the Children of Israel fell on their faces and cried out: "The Lord, He is God! The Lord, He is God!"')[7]

'The fire burns hot and mighty, swallowing up the mountain. I am listening, yet I do not hear God in the smoke, the ash, or the fire.'

---

7. See 1 Kings 18:20-40.

With patience. With perseverance. With compassion, Elijah stands, waits, and prays the fervent prayer of selfless struggle. And all the while, he listens for the Father's voice.

Patience. Perseverance. Compassion. The heartbeat of the believer's prayer. Surely, through these three, sandwiched within the sacredness of secret solitude, we become transformed to the likeness of Jesus Christ. And we no longer want to flee from the journey of prayerful suffering but, rather, to embrace those who suffer in the grip of Earth's web, and wrap them in compassionate prayer.

Without a doubt, the prayer of struggle is the least worn path the praying heart chooses to travel, for it is lined with the sharp shells and splintered glass of a Christ-devoted life. But it is a path necessary for spiritual growth, painful as it is. For it is the path traveled by Jesus Christ, Himself, behind us, before us, beside us.

So, don't give up, Elijah! For just when we are about to give up the struggle of compassionate encounter, just when our prayerful patience and perseverance is severely tested by the earthquakes, winds, and fires of life....

God speaks to us in a gentle whisper.

Questions for Group Study

1. Have you ever sought solitude and rest in prayer only to be drawn into 'the prayer of the struggling heart'? If so, please describe.

2. Define the word 'compassion.' Do you agree that compassion in prayer is 'the root, stem, and bloom of ministry through Christ to the world's others'? Why or why not?

3. Henri Nouwen writes: 'In and through solitude we do not move away from people, ... we move closer to them through compassionate ministry.' Name a time that solitude has led you to pray for others in need.

4. I compared the Christian's world to a spider's web. What other analogies could you use to describe our link with a world in pain, with a world that needs Christ?

5. Discuss the following statements:

    a. The prayer of the struggling heart. Does this prayer of our heart, this prayer too deep for words, touch the heart of God?

    b. Do our persistent prayers ever change the heart and mind of God? Why or why not?

    c. 'Does God respond to our prayers of struggle and sometimes choose to intervene?' (Have you ever had an experience where God directly intervened? If so, please describe.)

6. Read Hebrews 4:16 and examine its meaning.

    a. What do you think the word 'boldly' means in this particular context? (In the original Greek, 'boldness' means 'not keeping anything back,' in other words, confessing everything to God.)

7. How do our prayers prayed for the world's unknown others change our own hearts and minds? Have you been involved in situations where prayer for another changed you? If so, please describe.

8. Ponder the meaning of this question: 'How else but through a broken heart may Lord Christ enter in?' Do you agree or disagree and why?

Suggestions for Personal Reflection

Plan a certain time each day, either alone or with other believers, and pray for the needs of the world's people.

· Pray for the unborn babies, that they may develop strong and healthy.

· Pray for the mothers-to-be that they may be provided with nourishment and medical assistance to produce healthy children.

- Pray for the world's children, their spiritual upbringing, their diet, their home life, their families, their educations.
- Pray especially for the children who suffer from malnutrition and homelessness, for those orphaned and abandoned and abused, for those with special physical-, mental-, and emotional-needs, for those who will grow up but fail to achieve their God-given potential.
- Pray for the world's families, for the world's leaders, for the world's elderly, for the world's sick and dying.
- Most of all, pray especially for all those without Jesus Christ, that they may know His love and receive Him into their hearts and lives.
- Deeply ponder Hebrews 4:16 and the meaning of 'boldness' in prayer. As a part of your daily devotional time, read slowly Psalm 139 and compare it with Hebrews 4:16 for greater understanding.
- Read 1 John 5:14-15. In the quietness of your heart, meditate on this verse and this question: 'Do I believe God hears my prayers?'

Six

God's Gentle Whisper

I will never forget August 9, 1983. It was the last morning of her life. My beloved grandmother lay in a hospital 300 miles from my Kentucky home. Heavy with child, and so near my date of delivery, I grieved that I could not be by her bedside.

Every day the previous week, I telephoned her, hoping to hear her gentle voice. Yet I was met with the same disheartening words: 'Mama cannot speak. She's still in the coma.'

On this morning, I try one last time. My uncle answers the phone.

'I'm sorry, Denise, Mama cannot speak,' he tells me. 'She's still in the....'

'Wait!' I interrupt. 'Will you please just put the phone to her ear? I have something I must tell her.'

He consents. And even though she will not hear me, I yearn to tell her one more time how much I dearly love her.

'I love you, Mama,' are the only words I say to her, for those are the words I want her to remember. Always.

I sit at the phone, and, for the next few seconds, I listen to the sounds of her deep quiet breathing. As I start to place the phone back within its cradle, I know I will forever wonder if she has heard my final words.

And then ... then I hear a whisper, a faint wee whisper from the one I thought too ill to answer. I press the phone tightly to my ear, and strain to hear her voice.

And, to the amazement of all around, she speaks. She whispers, clear and sweet, six simple words that will echo within my ears throughout eternity ... "I know you love me, 'Nisey."

The Savior's Quiet Arrival

The year was around 3 BC. A young virgin cradled within her tender arms her newborn child. She was little more than a child herself.

The Jewish world had awaited a Savior, a Deliverer from God who would save them from sin's bondage. They watched. They listened. They prayed. And they waited for the Promised One to come.

They anticipated a mighty king, adorned with jeweled crown and purple robes of royal resplendence. They expected Him to enter their world on a team of swift white horses, an army of five-star generals marching close behind Him. They envisioned their king victoriously slashing the wrist of the reigning Romans and forever residing upon Jerusalem's regal throne.

But God did not arrive armored with horse and army. He did not overthrow the governing heads of state. He did not set up His own great kingdom, headquartered in Jerusalem with His staff of majestic generals.

Instead, God came with a whisper. He arrived a baby, tender and vulnerable, a child sustained and nourished by the warm milk of a peasant girl's breast. He came not by horse, but by donkey. He came not to a lofty throne, but to lowly manger. He arrived surrounded by shepherds, not soldiers. Scraggly shepherds who stooped, soiled and smelly, before His infant feet.

God, in His own time, in His own unexpected way, parted the curtain of time and space, and stepped gently into human history, history that would never again be the same.

But human hearts were not prepared for His quiet coming. Most of humanity missed God's arrival as they gazed prayerfully toward heaven and awaited a mighty King Messiah.

The God of Surprises

God is the God of surprises. When we expect Him to shout, He whispers. When we expect Him to whisper, He shouts. Sometimes He answers our prayers in flashy foil-wrapped packages adorned with bright streamers and bows. And sometimes He wraps his answers in plain brown paper. We have no trouble hearing Him when he responds to our prayers with a trumpet's blast. But the gentle whispers? How easily we can miss them, overlook them, lest we press the phone tightly to our ear, lest we continually pray the prayer of the expectant heart, the heart always watching and listening for God's surprises. A heart prepared to receive Him.

How God must have enjoyed surprising Elijah! Elijah stood on the mountain and he truly expected to hear God's call behind the quake, His roar within the wind, His shout above the flame.

But God spoke to him with a whisper. An unexpected whisper. And only because Elijah had tuned his heart to the heart of God, and, with all his strength listened, did he hear God's soft answer.

When Elijah was an old man, God had yet another surprise for him. He told Elijah to make one last journey. Young prophet-in-training, Elisha, walked with Elijah, and God led them to Bethel, then to Jericho, and then to the Jordan River.

Perhaps while they walked, Elijah listened for God's whisper. Perhaps Elijah strained his ear in expectation of God's gentle calling: 'Come home now, dear Elijah. You've completed the work I gave you to do.' Perhaps when Elijah's legs grew tired or when he faltered a step or two, he wondered when God would allow him to lie down and close his eyes in death's quiet slumber.

But just when Elijah expected to hear God's soft whisper calling him home ... SURPRISE, ELIJAH!

God sent from heaven a whirlwind of forceful fury, a chariot aglow with bright blazing fire, and a fleet of fast flaming horses to chauffeur Elijah directly into the arms of God! What a way to go!

God's Whisper in a Heart Beat

Around 30–33 AD Jesus is arrested, betrayed by His own chosen disciple. Peter, sword in hand, stands ready to do battle. When arresting soldiers grab Jesus, Peter pulls out a sword and slices off the ear of the High Priest's servant. Jesus rebukes Peter, and with a touch of his hand, replaces and heals the servant's severed ear. Before the night is over, Peter and the disciples will run away in fear.

Three crosses shade a mountaintop, a mountain shaped like a human skull. Jesus Christ hangs by spiked hands and feet between two seasoned thieves. A crown of sharp thorns cuts deep and encircles His bleeding brow. He says little. His agony is great. Above Him mocks a handmade sign: 'Jesus, King of the Jews.'

The executioners and religious zealots stand jeering at the base of the cross. If only they knew that the Creator, Himself, had just given His life, His blood, His last breath, for His wayward creation. If only they knew that God, Himself, had become a man, arms and legs, heart and lungs, intellect and talents – a man who, for our sake, had chosen to taste life as we live it, laughter and tears, joy and sorrows, birth and death.

But before He dies, Jesus whispers sweet words that will echo in our ears throughout eternity. 'Father, forgive them,'[1] and 'It is finished.'[2]

But God refuses to allow His Son to die quietly. Messiah's death does not whisper. Messiah's death shouts. The very universe responds to His death with screams of retribution as the sun, moon, and stars hide their faces and cover the earth with an intense blanket of unexplained darkness. Beneath the foreboding blanket, the earth quakes, rocks break apart, and long-time graves are disturbed and opened.

The death of our Lord is announced with a shout. On the third day of His death, something happens. Something mysterious. Something miraculous. Something that will cause humankind to marvel for the next 2000 years and beyond. Jesus Christ stands up alive and leaves His place of burial. He arises from the tight fist of death.

Enter trumpets! Enter angel chorus lines! Enter cymbals! Enter reporters and photographers from CNN! The *New York Times* early morning headlines will read: 'Christ Has Risen from the Dead!' 'Christ, Victorious Over Grave!' 'King of Jews Defeats Evil One!'

Hardly.

Christ's resurrection, the single one act of history that guarantees our divine destiny, that determines life and death itself, was announced with a whisper. To a couple of women and a group of disbelieving, bemoaning disciples.

Truly, God is the God of surprises!

Through God's gentle whispers – His Christmas Whisper, and His Whisper on Easter morning – God speaks to us His eternal words of love, of grace, of freedom from sin's bondage.

'I love you, dear child,' He whispers to you and me, for those are the words He wants us to remember. Always.

As we look at our Lord Jesus, as we witness His willingness to suffer human life and human death, to carry our cross for

---

1. Luke 23:34.
2. John 19:30.

us to the Place of the Skull, we can answer Him with six simple words of absolute certainty: 'I know you love me, Lord.'

Questions for Group Study

1. Name six ways we can prepare our hearts to hear God's gentle whispers? (How can we prepare our hearts to live in expectation and wonderment?)

2. Why is God the 'God of surprises'? Have you enjoyed God's surprises in your own life? If so, please explain.

3. Do you ever ponder the miracle of birth, of growth, of sunrise, of a flower's bloom, of a single breath of air, of a healthy heartbeat?

   a. Consider ways we can begin to take more appreciative notice of these everyday miracles in our lives.

   b. Consider ways we can instill a sense of prayerful gratitude to God for His creation and goodness in the lives of our children. (You might consider reading my book, *Teach Your Children to Pray*, as well as the book my husband, Timothy, and I coauthored together: *Our Dear Child*, both published by Christian Focus Publications.)

4. Why is prayer like 'the marvel of a heartbeat, the mystery of a breath, the miracle of a birth'? Describe what prayer means personally to you.

Suggestions for Personal Reflection

Discover ways that you can prepare your heart to see and enjoy God's surprises.

· Be aware of small things in life, such as a spider spinning a web or a wild flower growing in your back yard, for God can speak to your heart through all things, big and small.

· Pay special attention to the events that envelop your life. Is God speaking to you through one of these events?

- Take time to sit quietly and listen for His still, small voice. Take time to enjoy His creation of nature, of changing seasons, of children, of elderly people. Pay close attention to the words they say to you.

- Ponder those times you have distinctively felt God speaking to you in a surprising way.

Section III

The Responsive Heart

(When to His whisper our listening heart responds,
we prepare to serve God.)

When Elijah heard it [God's gentle whisper], he pulled his
cloak over his face and went out and stood at the mouth
of the cave.

(1 Kings 19:13)

SEVEN

STANDING AT THE MOUTH OF THE CAVE

Lucy reaches for the doorknob of the large old wardrobe. She expects it to be locked, but to her surprise, the knob turns. She opens the heavy door and, like any other ordinary child of curiosity, she peers inside. Stepping bravely, but slowly, into the mysterious darkness, sweet scents of cedar tease her nose and old moth balls crunch beneath her toes.

Outside the wardrobe play Peter, Edmund, and Susan. Downstairs in the library, the owner of the great English manse, an old English professor with 'shaggy white hair,' studies yet another thick volume.

Inside the closet Lucy lingers, walking ever so slowly and searching in vain for the wardrobe's back wall. But, alas! The wardrobe has no end. As she passes cautiously through, she meets unexpected rays of sunlight and the soft touch of snow upon her small young face.

Lucy soon discovers she has entered a new world, a world invisible and unknown to adults, a world full of mystery, wonder, and expectation, a world far away from the old professor's English manse.

Lucy has entered Narnia!

Narnia soon becomes Lucy's favorite secret place, a place where she finds rare surprises and delightful adventures, a world far more fascinating, far more beautiful, far more remarkable than the visible world in which she lives. How she wants to stay there, never again to leave!

Lucy's frequent and extended visits to Narnia change her as it introduces her to a world she didn't know existed, a world she can no longer live without. Time controls no part of Narnia, for there time stands still. What seems hours spent in Narnia's time, proves only minutes in Earth's time.

With Narnia deeply embedded in her heart and mind, Lucy goes about her ordinary days of school and work, but Narnia is never far away from her thoughts.

Eventually, Lucy introduces Peter, Edmund, and Susan to the delights of Narnia. Separately and together, the children visit Narnia many times throughout their childhood. But no matter how often they frequent it, Narnia never loses its mysterious enchantment, and the children never lose their love for this, their new-found world.

And the old professor – the old white-haired professor? Well, he knew much more than he professed to know, for he always met the children (when they returned from their Narnian adventures) with a smile on his lips and a twinkle in his eye.

God's Wondrous World

Of course, Narnia is an imaginary land that comes directly from the incredibly creative mind of C. S. Lewis as he captures the children's exciting adventures in his books, <u>The Chronicles of Narnia</u>.[1] (The heirloom wardrobe, upon which the book is based, stood in Lewis's own boyhood home. Lewis and his

---

1. C. S. Lewis, *The Chronicles of Narnia: The Lion, the Witch and the Wardrobe* (New York: Collier Books, 1950).

brother, Warren, would crawl into the wardrobe on rainy days and tell stories. It is now housed (along with Lewis's desk, his dining room table, his pipe, his pen, his chipped brown teapot and tall cup with a picture of a hunting scene) in the Marion E. Wade Center at Wheaton College, Wheaton, Illinois. If you have opportunity to visit Wheaton's Wade Center, you'll see a typed note posted on the door of the wardrobe. It reads amusingly: 'Enter at your own risk!' Recently, Narnia became a household word thanks to Hollywood's script-writers, actors, and big screens. I must admit, that, with the exception of some pretty scary well-teethed wolves, the film ('The Chronicles of Narnia: The Lion, the Witch and the Wardrobe') worked! It caused a lot of parents and children to learn more about Narnia and Aslan, the Lion.

I first read C. S. Lewis' *Narnia* series during the mid-1970s, when I lived and worked and went to school in Cambridge, Massachusetts. The books mesmerized me as I commuted long hours by subway and bus in and out of Boston's Back Bay. One night, as I rode a Boston bus from work to home, I became so enthralled with Aslan, the lion-Christ figure, I sailed three stops past my regular bus stop! When I finally closed the book and stepped off the bus, I had no idea where I was! I put the book under my arm and had to walk more than two miles back to my house.

The Wardrobe

I find much remarkable resemblance between the large old wardrobe that opened to Lucy the wondrous world of Narnia, and my own private prayer-closet that opens to me the wondrous world of God.

For instance...

The door to my prayer-closet is never locked but opens easily. And when I step into its majestic mystery, I find my Father waiting there to welcome me. My prayer-closet has become my favorite place to go, to tarry, a place far more fascinating, far more beautiful, far more welcoming, and far more remarkable than the visible world I know.

Perhaps the visible world that seems so real is not the real world at all but a sort of 'shadow-world,' a shadow of the real world. Perhaps it is this invisible world, where we meet God in quiet privacy, where you and I as believers in Christ will spend all eternity ... perhaps this world we cannot see is truly the 'real world.'

Like Lucy, when I visit my invisible world, I come back changed. I come back renewed, refreshed, rewarded with a heart more anchored in love in God's own heart.

Before I met Christ, I never knew this world of prayer existed. Now, many years later, God's open wardrobe has become my favorite passageway to a world I can no longer live without. And no matter how busy my day, no matter how hectic my schedule, my precious prayer-closet times are so deeply embedded in my heart and mind, that the Lord is never far away. It is the prepared heart that holds onto God's presence between the times of quiet solitude, between prayer-closet times.

How often I go into the Narnia of prayer with my hands empty. But I always come out with my hands full, full of God's joy and rich blessings. How often I go in with my brief case full, full of heartaches and headaches, worries, deadlines, and fears. But I find I can leave my brief case there, and come back relieved of the load with which I struggled.

When I step into my prayer-closet, I leave Earth's restrictive clock, and I move most willingly and freely into God's time. In His mysterious presence, time seems to stand still. No matter how many times I visit the delightful world of my Father, the prayer-closet never loses its mystery and wonder and awe. And I never lose my love for this, my new-found world.

For inside those closet doors, those doors that open to me such perfect fellowship with my Father, I celebrate!

I celebrate Jesus Christ and the remarkable gift of His love for me, of His life to me.

I celebrate the beauty around me, beauty created for me to enjoy by the loving Creator, Himself.

I celebrate life, with its amazing heartbeat and breath, with its wondrous miracle of birth and bountiful new life.

I celebrate the little girl within me who wakes up in the mornings with 'a prayer on her lips and a song in her heart,' as my grandfather taught me to say. I am the child who still enters the prayer-closet with wide-eyed curiosity and wonder and expectation of surprise.

And I celebrate this priceless, precious gift of prayer, the honor of entering into the King's Royal Chambers as His beloved daughter, a member of His family.

Truly, prayer is a welcome haven from the turmoil all around me.

Oh, that I can introduce the prayer-closet to the Peters and Edmunds and Susans of this world! Oh, that I may personally bring them to the One who holds the mysteries of the universe in the palm of His hand, a hand plenteous with power, a hand laden with love ... for you, for me, for them, forever.

The Prayer of the Prepared Heart

I love my prayer-closet times, those times I can concentrate without interruption on God's goodness and generosity.

'We have to know someone before we can truly love them,' writes Brother Lawrence. 'In order to know God, we must think about Him often. And once we get to know Him, we will think about Him even more often, because where our treasure is, there also is our heart.'[2]

To know Him better, to love Him more, I delight to sit in His tender presence and ponder the mysteries of faith and life. I love to open the book, His Word, and run my fingers over the life-giving words, words that centuries of Christians have read

---

2. Brother Lawrence, *The Practice of the Presence of God* (Springdale, PA: Whitaker House, 1982), p. 46.

and treasured. I could pitch my tent in Narnia and live there forever, enjoying and reveling in the invisible world where I and my Father are one.

But bills must be paid, children fed, letters faxed, laundry washed, bathrooms scrubbed, kids car-pooled, life's various matters attended to. From within the walls of my quiet solitude, I hear the impatient whine of a 27-cubic-foot refrigerator that waits to be refilled. Reluctantly, I leave the precious silence and reenter the chaos of Shadow-World. Once again I must step into the loud merry-go-round society that runs in meaningless circles like plaster-of-Paris horses with wide painted smiles and glazed glass eyes.

But I enter Shadow-World with a heart that never ceases to pray the prayer of the prepared heart, a heart that prays in spite of the chaos enclosing it.

I am learning that 'ceaseless interior prayer is a continual yearning of the human spirit towards God.'[3]

Above the noise and endless chaos, my human spirit strains to listen, to hear the gentle voice that calls me 'come,' a voice so easily drowned out by the incessant roar of Shadow-World, a voice that only a prayer-prepared heart can hear.

Shadow-World, with its duties and responsibilities, is somewhat like the valley that lies between the mountaintop experiences of prayer.

Some years ago, when my husband and I worked and attended school in Cambridge, Massachusetts, we occasionally climbed into our old '69 faded green Plymouth Satellite and drove through the mountains of Vermont.

Reveling about our break from books and typewriters, we stopped often, unpacked lunch and snacks, and sat on

---

3. Henri J. M. Nouwen, *The Way of the Heart* (New York: Ballantine Books, 1981), pp. 67, 68.

the quiet mountaintops to eat. Long after the peanut butter sandwiches disappeared, Timothy and I sat still and gazed silently out over the rows of rolling green hills, each hill with its own valley, each valley with its own village, each village with its own newly painted white church steeple.

Deep passionate prayer poured forth freely from my heart during those rare outings, those quiet hours of husband-and-wife solitude when Vermont's warm sunshine and gentle white clouds revealed beauty immeasurable and unspeakable.

But the dictates of time and the everyday demands of life told us we couldn't stay in quiet solitude upon a distant Vermont mountaintop. We had to come back to the world of dirty streets, tuition bills, broken water pipes, and unreasonable deadlines ... the world where prayer can so easily be crowded out by the long lists of that day's 'to do's.'

Even Jesus, Himself, had to come down from the mountaintop, refasten His sandals, roll up His sleeves, and continue the work God gave Him to do.

Pray Without Ceasing

How easily we can be drawn to prayer atop a Vermont mountain or within the enveloping solitude of our secret place. But how difficult prayer can be during the ticket-paying, toilet-cleaning, timecard-punching 'mean times' of life, those times when we must step out of god's time and back into Earth's demanding schedule.

I believe prayer is vital to our lives as Christians. To live a Christian life without prayer is like trying to live a physical life without air.'[4] The Apostle Paul urges us to 'pray without ceasing' (1 Thess. 5:17). Jesus tells His hard-working disciples to 'come with me by yourselves to a quiet place and get some rest' (Mark 6:31).

If prayer is as important to our spiritual lives as breathing is to our physical lives....

If Paul asks us to remain in prayer continually, never ceasing....

If Jesus wants His followers to find a quiet place of solitude and rest in prayer....

If, if, if, for the 21st century Christian, then becomes how, how, how?

How can we spend a lifetime in prayer and fellowship with our Father when we have so much to do, so many places to go, so many needs to fulfill?

How can you and I, like Elijah, stand patiently outside the mouth of the cave and listen for God's gentle calling in the midst of earthquake, wind, and fire confusion that constantly distract us?

How can we so tune our hearts to the heart of God, that even when we are encircled by society's chaos, our hearts are prepared to feel His presence and hear His voice?

Even during – especially during – those times when ...

We fill our trash cans full of garbage and the truck doesn't run...

We mail our bills, due yesterday, and the carrier doesn't pass...

Our key-holding teenager runs out the back toward the family car, while our toddlers runs out the front, diaper-less...

The simmering stew has firmly attached itself to the bottom of the pot, and dinner guests are ringing the bell.

In 1710 Matthew Henry wrote: 'A gold thread of heart-prayer must run through the web of the whole Christian life.'[4]

How can you and I weave any kind of purposeful, passionate prayer within and throughout the ordinary hours of our busy

---

4. Matthew Henry, "A Method for Prayer" (Chester, MA: [copy of original pamphlet dated March 25, 1710]).

every-days? Pray as we breathe? Pray without ceasing? Escape to the mountaintop to pray in the middle of the day?

Impossible?

***

We are women whose schedules are governed by time, husbands, homes, children, aging parents, office bosses, unbalanced checkbooks, self-employed businesses, and life-health-medical-house-car-dental-burial insurance payments.

Most Christian women I know rise early in the morning, hit the floor running, keep an Olympic track pace throughout the day, and don't stop running, hauling, commuting, chauffeuring, delivering, car pooling, and helping until late that night. In fact, I believe that if the Proverbs 31 woman were expected to carry the work and family load the average woman of today manages, she would throw up her hands and go back to bed.

Christian women today are deeply involved in the nurture of their families, in the maintenance of homes, in the work places, in their churches, in their neighborhoods and communities.

As believers in Christ, we want to reach out to those who hurt and grieve, to those who are hungry and cold, to the unchurched, to the lost, to the troubled. Yet, we are limited, so limited by dwindling time and energy in light of all that desperately needs to be done.

Pray without ceasing? Can it be done? How different our every-days would be if we could keep our hearts forever focused upon God, always listening, always prepared and ready to respond to His divine instructions.

The Priority of Prayer

Jesus made prayer and fellowship with the Father the priority in His life. Whether He hammered a nail into a board, reached out to heal a man born blind, lifted small children upon His lap, or took a whip to the Temple money changers, He knew that God was only a heart's whisper away. The Father and Son had unbroken communion throughout the days of Jesus' life on Earth. Jesus kept His heart focused on His Father while He worked, while He traveled, while He ministered.

Christ used to spend nights in prayer (Luke 6:12). He often rose a great while before day in order to have unbroken communion with His Father (Mark 1:35). The great crises of His life and ministry were preceded by special prayer (e.g. Luke 5:16), 'He Himself would often slip away to the wilderness and pray,' a statement that indicated a regular habit. Both by word and example He impressed upon His disciples the importance of solitude in prayer (Mark 6:46, Luke 9:28).[5]

I watched my grandmother follow Jesus' example of prayer, committing her time and energy to God, and praying that He would reveal His will to her concerning how she spent her hours. Mama began each day with prayer, ended each day with prayer, and wove the golden thread of prayer within and throughout all the hours of her day. In her work, in her walk, in her relationships with others, in her grief, and in her pain, the radiance of Christ shone from within her heart onto her precious face.

Mama discovered early in life the secret of unceasing communion. For she discovered that God is not only above us, below us, around us, and beside us. God, the Holy Spirit, lives within us. He is as close as our heartbeats, as near as our breathing. Our bodies are His Temple, the place in which He resides. We might not always be aware of His presence, but we are never without His presence. So caught up in this merry-go-round life, we can sometimes forget the closeness of God. But Christ lives in the chapel of our hearts, a sort of 'portable prayer-closet' we take with us, a secret place of prayer that's only a thought away.

Mama never sat upon a Vermont mountaintop to pray, but she prayed continually within the sanctuary of her heart.

---

5. J. Oswald Sanders, *Spiritual Leadership* (Chicago, IL: Moody Press, 1967/1980), p 106.

In the quietness of her soul, she lived on the mountaintop, in unending communion with God. Within the chapel of her heart, she came to know God, to love God, and to serve God.

Can't you tell the people who live on the mountaintop, those who dwell in conversation with God within the chapel of their hearts?

> Oh, their problems aren't any different. And their challenges are just as severe. But there is a stubborn peace that enshrines them.... A serenity that softens the corners of their lips. A contagious delight sparkling in their eyes. And in their hearts reign a fortress-like confidence that the valley can be endured, even enjoyed, because the mountain is only a decision away.[6]

All Things Become Prayer

Surely, as the gold thread of prayer weaves itself in and out and throughout our ordinary hours, God's presence enriches us through those prayerful pauses and puts meaning into the most mundane duties of our days. Even though we cannot see it now, those strands of shining gold are becoming a splendid work of art, weaving our everyday hours into the rich tapestry of a lifetime devoted to God. And God's loving fingerprints are braided deep within the tapestry of our lives, adding delicate design and delight to our every-days.

> To realize the intimacy of the Master's touch upon all the minutiae of my affairs, to experience His hand guiding, leading, directing in every detail of each day, is to enter a delight words cannot describe.[7]

When we put our hands in our Father's hand as we go about our hours, whatever we think, whatever we do, whatever we say, will be a form of prayer for us, and ministry for others.

---

6. Lucado, *The Applause of Heaven*, p. 23.
7. Keller, *A Shepherd Looks at The Good Shepherd and His Sheep*, p. 171.

The morning walk with a child through spring's first tiny wildflowers...

> The beautifully-resolved conflict with our co-worker...
> The homemade bread given to our elderly neighbor...
> The ear we kindly lend to a nonstop talker...
> The money we place in our church offering envelope...
> The little scraped knees we bandage and kiss...
> The courtesy we show a driver in non-moving traffic...
> The kind words we speak to a rude waitress...
> The way in which we gratefully view the evening sunset...
> The way we invite God to direct our thoughts ... thoughts

true and noble and right, pure, admirable and excellent and lovely, praiseworthy....[8]

When all things abide in Christ, all things become prayer, all things become opportunities for ministry, and the touch of Christ is upon each hour of our days, blessing it, enriching it.

Our hearts will know a strange, but beautiful, kind of peace, for the heart at peace is the heart prepared that practices the continual presence of Jesus Christ throughout the most ordinary days.

The God of the Second Chance

The chapel of our hearts also provides opportunity for regular confession of wrongdoing. We confess our wrongs, and even before He hears our confessions, God has already forgiven us through Christ.

God forgives us when, during the course of our everyday, we stumble and fall, when we make mistakes in relationships, when we pursue those thoughts and those things unworthy of God's presence within us. He allows us to get back up on our feet and start over again.

J. Oswald Sanders, in his book, *Spiritual Leadership*, puts this concept of forgiveness in a poignant way:

---

8. Philippians 4:8 (NKJV).

A study of bible characters reveals that most of those who made history ... failed at some point, and some of them drastically, but [they] refused to continue lying in the dust. Their very failure and repentance secured to them a more ample conception of the grace of God. They learned to know Him as the God of the second chance to His children who had failed Him – and the third chance, too."[9]

Many times God has picked me up when I stumbled, brushed off my dusty clothes, kissed my forehead, and, through His gift of grace, given me a second chance. And a third chance, too!

Does unceasing prayer and fellowship with the Father take priority in our every-days? Jesus gave prayer first place in His day, in His life, and Jesus is our example. While responsibilities to those we love must be met, our relationship to God, our responsibility to Him, must always come first. For with those we love we will walk but a mile. But with God, who is Love, we will walk an eternity.

Dwelling in the prayer-chapel of our hearts as we go about our day will develop within us a prayerful attitude. A prayerful attitude will prepare our hearts to hear God's call when He whispers to us. For the forever walk with God, the walk that lasts throughout eternity, begins the moment you and I decide to give Him our lives, all our earthly hours, and to wait at the mouth of the cave of our hearts to respond to His call that beckons us 'come.'

And when He calls, let us expect a surprise, for His soft voice will change our lives, no matter who we are, no matter where we are.

Do you remember Andrew and Simon, Zacchaeus and the nameless Samaritan woman at the well? Christ's call changed their lives forever.

Christ looked for Andrew and Simon and found them fishing on the shores of a lake. 'Come, Andrew. Come, Simon,' Jesus called. And they followed Him and found a new vocation.

---

9. Sanders, p. 163.

Christ looked for Zacchaeus and found him perched high in the limbs of a tree. 'Come, Zacchaeus,' Jesus called. And Zacchaeus climbed down and found a new heart.

Christ looked for a woman by a Samaritan well and found one shunned, sad, and without hope. 'Come, dear one,' Jesus called. And she drank from His cup of Living Water and found a new life and a new mission.

Listen carefully, for in our noisiest hours, Christ may call to you, to me. He may call to us through the closeness of a grandmother's shoulder, the innocent face of an inner city child, a summer morning's gentle shower, fresh okra frying in a cast iron skillet, a hillside covered with tender young pines, a seashore alive with silver-winged seagulls, the miracle of a baby's birth, or a common spider that weaves her web outside our bedroom windows.

Listen, let us listen with the ears of our hearts, hearts prepared to hear God's voice. For it may come at unpredictable times, in unpredictable ways. Then let us follow ... follow Him when He petitions us to come.

'The incredibly beautiful relationship between the Shepherd and His sheep can be and only is possible provided the sheep hear His voice, are known of Him in intimate oneness, and so follow Him in quiet, implicit confidence.'[10]

As we tarry in the chapel of our hearts, the relationship you and I now share with God will be enriched and strengthened with time ... until that time, when we can step into the large old wardrobe ... with its scent of cedar and its crunch of moth balls ... where time no longer rules.

And when that time comes, let us enter Narnia with a smile on our lips and a twinkle in our eyes, for we can finally stay there, in that place that has no end, never again to leave.

---

10. Keller, *A Shepherd Looks at The Good Shepherd and His Sheep*, p. 165.

Questions for Group Study

1. 'Perhaps the visible world that seems so real, is not the real world at all, but simply a sort of "shadow-world," a shadow of the real world. Perhaps it is the world that is invisible, where we meet God in quiet privacy, where you and I as believers in Christ will spend all eternity ... perhaps this world, this world we cannot see, is truly the "real world."'

   a. Do you understand the full meaning of this statement? Please explain it.

2. 'It is the prepared heart that holds onto God's presence between the times of quiet solitude, between prayer-closet times.'

   a. Voice your opinion of that statement.
   b. List five ways we can prepare our hearts to 'practice God's presence' between the times of the prayer-closet.

3. From within your own prayer-closet walls, what do you celebrate?

   a. List what you are most thankful for today.
   b. List what is most meaningful to you today.
   c. List those things you are most concerned about, those things that desperately need your prayers.

4. Do you agree with Henri Nouwen that 'ceaseless interior prayer is a continual yearning of the human spirit towards God'?

   a. What does this statement mean to you?
   b. Has it tested true in your own life? If so, how?

5. Do you believe that prayer is vital to our lives as Christians today? Why? Please state several reasons.

6. Contemplate and discuss: 'How can we spend a lifetime in prayer and fellowship with our Father when we have so much to do, so many places to go, so many needs to fulfill?'

   a. Name some ways not listed in the chapter, ways that you personally have found meaning in your own life.

7. Is it realistic to believe that we, as busy Christian women, can learn to 'pray without ceasing'? How?

   a. Please share some meaningful and helpful ideas.

8. Read Colossians 4:2. What does this verse say to us in regard to how and when we pray?

9. How can you and I follow Jesus' example and make prayer a priority in our lives?

10. Read Mark 1:35, 6:46; Luke 5:16, 6:12, 9:28. What do these verses tells us about the practice of prayer in Jesus' life?

Suggestions for Personal Reflection

· Read Psalm 66:18. Meditate upon the concept of forgiveness as described in this chapter by J. Oswald Sanders, in his book *Spiritual Leadership*.

   · Ask God to forgive your sins, the hidden ones as well as the visible ones.

   · Pray that God will help you to forgive those who have mistreated or betrayed or abused you.

   · Begin each prayer you pray asking God for His generous forgiveness.

EIGHT

THE SERVANT'S HEART

Several years ago, my friend, Scotti, only 33 years old at the time, fainted as she climbed stairs on a hot July day. That's when her nightmare began.

A pastor's wife, Scotti had three children, a six-week-old baby, Jondelyn, a kindergartener, Scott, and an older daughter, Andrea. For no apparent reason, her blood pressure shot up and her heart enlarged.

Final diagnosis: Primary Pulmonary Hypertension.

After several weeks of unsuccessful medical treatment, Scotti's doctor told her he could do nothing more.

'How long will I live?' she asked him.

He shook his head. 'Some people with PPH live six weeks; others can go on several years. There's no way to know.'

Scotti didn't want to die. 'I have so much left to do. I want to see my children grow up. I love my husband Jon.'

Jon took the news hard. 'Is there nothing, nothing at all we can do?' he asked the doctor.

The doctor gave him only one ray of hope. 'There is the possibility that a heart and lung transplant can save her,' he told Jon. 'That is, if Scotti will agree to it and if we can find a donor.'

Church members, family, and friends immediately encircled Scotti with prayer. Jon and Scotti flew to Pittsburgh, and put their name on the organ donor list there.

Eight months elapsed.

No donor.

They drove to Birmingham, Alabama, and put their name on a second organ donor list. Then, with a multitude of those who loved them, they prayed, they waited, and they hoped, as time ticked off like a broken clock.

A call finally came from the hospital.

'Scotti, we have a heart/lung donor. Get everything ready to come today. Wait by the phone and I'll call you back.'

Jon called a deacon in their church, a former pilot, who had offered to arrange a private flight. With suitcase in hand, they waited and waited and waited. They waited all day by the phone. At 4:00 the call came.

'I'm sorry, Scotti. The donor has an infection. We can't use his lungs.'

Scotti's condition worsened as more time passed. Two years had passed since her doctor had diagnosed PPH. No donor was in sight. But the prayers continued – urgent prayers – prayed on behalf of Scotti.

On the morning of August 15, 1990, the Organ Transplant Coordinator from the University of Alabama Hospital called again. 'Scotti, we have a heart/lung donor. Get everything read to come today.'

Scotti placed her hand over her failing heart. 'Tonight,' she said aloud, as if trying to make the almost unthinkable seem believable. 'Tonight, I'll have a new heart and lungs.'

Scotti barely had time to unpack her suitcase before the surgery began. Lovingly, she took out the photo of her family, the lace bookmark Scott had made for her at Christmas, and the little wooden box Andrea gave her on her birthday, the birthday she thought might be her last.

The surgery went well. But three weeks later, something happened. Scotti developed a viral infection, and her lungs filled with fluid.

The situation was serious. Her fluid-filled lungs could receive only 30 percent of the oxygen her body needed to sustain her life. Doctors could give her family no assurance that Scotti would live. The head resident came into her room and prayed with Scotti and Jon.

The church organized a 24-hour-a-day prayer chain and prayed ardently, unceasingly, for Scotti, as she lay in the hospital's Critical Intensive Care Unit.

They prayed, they waited, they hoped. And to the relief of all, a few days later Scotti's lungs began to clear. Day after day, x-rays showed a slight improvement, until sixty-six days after the surgery, Scotti was well enough to be released from the hospital. With a new heart and lungs, Scotti walked into the front door of her home on her thirty-sixth birthday, two weeks before Thanksgiving, eager to begin life anew.

'The experience has taught me to depend completely on God,' Scotti recalls. 'He showed His love through our church and family and friends who supported us continually with prayer. And God showed His love to us through an anonymous mother who, through the generous donation of her son's heart and lungs, turned his tragic death into the gift of new life, the gift that enabled this grateful mother to return home to her husband and children.'

The Transformed Heart

Scotti Doler was not the only one who received a new heart. Those faithful believers who prayed with her, for her, who so unselfishly held her for long months before the Father, also received new heart, servants' hearts filled with love. Love unfathomable. The love, the heart of Christ, Himself.

Prayers of intercession, prayed from the depths of our hearts, change our hearts. The natural heart, so preoccupied with self, transforms and becomes, instead, the heart engaged with others. The 'self-oriented' heart matures into the 'other-oriented' heart. The Shepherd's heart and our praying hearts become one, beating within our breasts on behalf of another who needs our prayers.

The self-giving servant cannot pray for another and, at the same time, maintain a selfish spirit. For the servant dies to self, the old self that lived only for self. She wants eagerly to give her new self to those whom Jesus loves, to those for whom Jesus has given Himself. When that happens, the natural heart, the selfish heart, is given the eyes of Christ, the gift of divine insight, and it can never again see the person in Earth's same dim light.

If the prayer of the struggling heart petitions God on behalf of the world's unknown others, the prayer of the servant's heart, the interceding heart, puts faces on those we hold in prayer. Intercessory prayer lifts to God, by name and need, those we envelop with prayer.

The Gift of Intercessory Prayer

Years ago, I heard a speaker deliver a moving speech urging the audience to join her crusade, a life-saving moment I whole-heartedly endorsed.

But her final request disturbed me. She told us: 'If you cannot volunteer your time and energy to this great cause – if you can't do anything else, then pray for us.'

I had heard those same words spoken before by well-meaning believers. 'If you can't do anything else ... then pray.'

Work, energy, time, money, blood, sweat, tears – nothing, nothing we can give another person can, in any way, equal the gift of service we give to them by praying for them. Intercessory prayer is the gift we give that remains unequaled in offering, in value.

When we pray for others, we show our love for our Savior, and we show our love for His sheep. No sweeter words can be said than those spoken to the Father on behalf of His child.

Whenever I close my eyes, I can see the slender form of my white-haired grandfather kneeling in prayer beside the plaid, family-room chair. It is one of my earliest and sweetest memories.

So regularly did he kneel there and pray for others, the chair's cloth arm was worn bare in the spot where he placed his steadying hand.

My grandparents spent most of their prayer time praying for others. As a skinny, pig-tailed girl, I remember my grandfather telling me that they 'called my name everyday in prayer.'

As I grew up, married, had children, and dealt with a legion of decisions and pressures, I was always aware of, and comforted by their loving petitions for me.

I now look back and realize that those were the dearest, most caring words Papa could ever say to me. Until his death in my thirty-sixth year, I always knew that no matter where in the world I was, no matter what situation I faced, no matter how I hurt or grieved, somewhere on a little farm in Rossville, Georgia, my grandparents were praying for me. It brought me a comfort and strength that nothing else could.

> Jesus said: 'Love the Lord your God with all your heart and with all your soul and with all your mind and with all your strength.... [And] love your neighbor as yourself. There is no commandment greater than these' (Mark 12:30-31).

Intercessory prayer is the very heart of prayer, the prayer that not only blesses the one prayed for, but blesses the one who prays as well.

> 'We are never more like Christ than in prayers of inter-cession.'[1]

---

1. Austin Phelps, *The Still Hours* (Carlisle, PA: The Banner of Truth Trust, 1974 [first published in 1859]), p. 80.

Does Jesus, Himself, not call our hearts to become servants' hearts, hearts that kneel before God on behalf of others? The God of Creation humbled Himself to become one of us, to serve us, and He calls us to follow His self-giving example.

> The greatest among you should be like the youngest, and the one who rules like the one who serves.... I am among you as one who serves (Luke 22:26-27).

How difficult is this servanthood concept for twenty-first century hearts! Our society instructs us to do the opposite: 'Blessed is she,' it teaches, 'who is influential and strong, powerful and ambitious, commanding and controlling, assertive and self-assured.'

'Dress for success!' it screams.

'Be Number One!' it advises.

'Climb your way to the top,' it encourages, 'no matter who you step on along the way up!'

Yet, Jesus issues an even stronger command to you and me, one much more difficult to do:

'Serve,' He says.

When Peter wanted to convey his love for Christ, he stated boldly: 'Lord, I am ready to go with You to prison and to death.' (Luke 22:33).

But Jesus gave Peter a harder task to prove his love.

> 'Peter,' Jesus said, 'Take care of My sheep; feed My lambs' (Paraphrased: See John 21:15-17.)

What better way to take care of, to minister to, and to nourish, support, and sustain those whom Jesus loves, than to intercede for them in prayer?

> 'The effective, fervent prayer of a righteous man avails much,' wrote the author of James (James. 5:16 NKJV).

An effective prayer is a functional, practical prayer – a specific need requested of the Father.

A fervent prayer is an impassioned prayer – an intense, zealous, eager prayer. We cannot enter the prayer-closet to pray for another with our hearts unconcerned, indifferent, or listless. In the Garden of Gethsemane before Jesus faced the cross, so fervent was His prayer for you and me, that Luke, the physician, notes: 'His sweat was like drops of blood falling to the ground' (Luke 22:44 [see Luke 22:39-53]).

The Poem of Prayer

Each night before I sleep, I lie in bed and study my 'prayer wall' of photos. Some are new; some are old; some are faded with age. But each person is precious to me, and each receives a special prayer before I close my eyes.

I love the people who look to me from my bedside wall. I pray for them with thoughts of love; I pray for them by need and name. But, a lifetime of friendship and love itself, cannot disclose the deepest needs of their hearts and souls. I can but know a few. The rest I must accept are known by God alone.

> For all those needs unknown to me,
> I ask that God will touch and tend,
> My silent prayers to Him I lift,
> The One Who is all-knowing.[2]

You see, a person's life is like a poem. A living, breathing poem.

What is a poem? It is a collection of simple everyday words – carefully chosen words – a word here, a word there, each painting a portrait, each denoting a thought, each conveying a concept. In poetry, a word is worth a thousand pictures.

A poem is like a small town's junkyard that whispers its unwritten history by the bits and pieces it leaves behind. Bits and pieces as of a puzzle, a puzzle that speaks unspoken volumes to those who will listen, to those who will look.

---

2. Denise George.

We listen and we see ...

A rusted tricycle and the life of a man who, as a toddler, once rode upon it ...

A pair of worn crutches and a tired old veteran with a wealth of war tales, remembered and shared ...

A dog-eared cookbook and a mother's devotion as day after day she loves and feeds those who gather at her table.

Such is a person like a poem. When we walk through a person's life, carefully and slowly, we see the puzzle of bits and pieces – bits of love and joy, pieces of hurt and sorrow. By listening, by looking, we can read volumes unspoken.

We listen and we see ...

The rusted tricycle of the child she never had ...

The worn crutches of a dream she had to forfeit ...

The dog-eared cookbook of a love she found and lost,

For each person's life is lived full and empty. And we are given but a stanza, never the full verse of her life.

But God knows her heart, in and out and throughout the sonnet of her soul. He knows every thought, every fear, every desire. He knows her gain and loss, her hope and dream, her secret love. He knows the ballad of her heart as He knows His own heart, without secret, without pretense, without the masquerade of a self-concealing mask.

Thus, we hold the face of the one we love before us, within our secret chambers. With words unspoken, but with words impassioned, we place this living, breathing poem of life at the faithful Father's feet.

Surely, 'the real business of [our] life as a saved soul is intercessory prayer,' the 'ministry of the interior.'[3]

---

3. Chambers, *If You Will Ask*, p. 172.

'If your heart is as My heart, then give Me your hand.'[4] Let us, together, hear anew Christ's words to me, to you.

'Take care of My sheep.'

'Feed My lambs.'

And when we care for, and when we feed those He entrusts, through prayer, to us ... we will be given new hearts, servants' hearts filled with love. Love unfathomable. The love, the heart, of Christ, Himself.

Questions for Group Study

1. Ponder this statement about intercessory prayer: 'Prayers of intercession, prayed from the depths of our hearts, change our hearts. The natural heart, so preoccupied with self, transforms and becomes, instead, the heart engaged with others.'

   a. Have you found this statement to be true? If so, in what ways?

2. Consider the word 'transformation.' What does it mean to you?

   a. Have you experienced a transforming time in your own life that you can share with a friend or group?

3. Describe the difference between these two prayers: The prayer of the struggling heart and the prayer of the servant's heart.

4. 'Work, energy, time, money, blood, sweat, tears – nothing, nothing we can give another person can, in any way, equal the gift of service we give to them by praying for them. Intercessory prayer is the gift we give that remains unequaled in offering, in value.'

   a. Do you regard the worth of intercessory prayer to be this vital to the Christian life? Why or why not?

5. 'We are never more like Christ than in prayers of intercession.'

---

4. Phrase quoted by John Wesley.

a. How do our prayers, by need and name, for others help us to become more like Christ? Discuss.

6. Can you describe in as few words as possible the meaning of 'the servant's heart.'

7. Read John 21:15-17. What do these verses mean to you?

8. This chapter compares a person's life to a poem. Can you think of other ways to describe a person's life as it relates to intercessory prayer?

9. Do you agree with this statement by Oswald Chambers concerning intercessory prayer: 'The real business of [our] life as a saved soul is intercessory prayer'? Please explain why or why not.

Suggestions for Personal Reflection

· In your quiet time, reread John 14:13-14 and meditate upon its meaning and its promise.

· Contemplate deeply Mark 11:24. Then pray for those you know and love, by name and need, with the promise of God in your heart that He will hear and answer your prayers prayed on behalf of others.

· Set aside a certain time each day to pray specifically for the needs of others. To pray the prayer without words, here are some suggestions:

· Write down your prayer request on a slip of paper. Then place it, along with others, in a small box. Daily, in your quiet time, reread the prayer requests you've written. After a certain amount of time has passed, go through the box and note the answered prayers.

· Keep a photo of those you pray for daily. Look at the photo as you think about and pray for that particular person. Ask God to lead you to pray for that person according to his or her present need.

· When an intercessory prayer need is urgent, write the need on a card and attach to your cabinet or refrigerator or desk or dashboard. During the day, use the card as a constant reminder to pray frequently for this person and her particular need.

· After you pray a prayer of intercession, consider writing a note to the person you have prayed for. Let her know of your prayers and love for her.

· As you pray for another, envision in your mind that the person for whom you are praying is kneeling and joining you in prayer.

NINE

THE SHEPHERD'S HEART

John Griffin adores his eight-year-old son, Greg. Father and son, they look alike, they walk alike, and they talk alike – of ships and seas and exotic places they will one day sail together. John's wife smiles as she listens to them dream aloud, long into the night, of faraway fantastic places.

On this warm spring day in 1937, John, the operator of one of the major railway drawbridges that crosses the Mississippi River, brings Greg to work with him. For the very first time, Greg watches with excitement as his father pulls a lever and raises the giant bridge to let a ship pass through. Then, with equal enthusiasm, Greg watches his father pull the lever that lowers the bridge to let a train pass over.

At noon, John raises the bridge and lets a ship pass through. Then he pats his son on the back. 'There won't be a train for a while,' he tells Greg. 'Want to see the deck?'

Greg shouts a hearty 'yes,' and father and son walk a few hundred feet down the catwalk and eat sack lunches on the bridge observation deck.

A golden sun warms the air and a gentle wind breezes along the river as John and Greg look out upon the water and talk of the magical places the ships might sail. Time stands still as father and son enjoy each other's company.

Suddenly, a sharp distant whistle startles their thoughts. John jumps to his feet and looks at his watch. The Memphis Express, the train that passes each day at 1:07, is speeding down the railway track ... and the bridge is raised!

'Stay here, Greg!' John shouts and races down the catwalk, climbs the ladder, and rushes into the control booth.

'Four hundred passengers are on that train,' he mutters to himself as he quickly places his hand on the lever to lower the mighty bridge. But just as he begins to pull the lever, he sees a horrible sight.

'Greg!' he screams. But Greg can't move. The young boy has tried to follow his dad. But he has slipped and fallen. Greg's left leg is firmly lodged in the gigantic gear box that operates the drawbridge.

John freezes. He knows that if he pulls the lever to lower the bridge, tons of grinding steel will slowly chew and crush Greg's small body. But he also knows that if he doesn't pull the lever, 400 passengers abroad the Memphis Express will be hurled to their deaths in the river below.

John sees a rope hanging in the corner of the control booth. 'Will it work?' he asks himself.

Gripped by panic, John plans his son's rescue. If only he can reach his son in time, he can use the rope to lower himself into the gears, free his son, climb back up the rope, race back to the control booth, and pull the lever.

John grabs the rope and scurries down the first few steps of the ladder toward his son. Then John hears the high-pitched train whistle again, shrieking much louder than before, now much closer than he had thought.

Too close to rescue his son.

His heart stabs with pain, his eyes fill with tears. Oh, how he loves his boy, his only son, caught beneath him in the drawbridge gears. But he knows only one thing to do. Four hundred passengers will be speeding across the track any second, and they are depending on John to have the drawbridge safely lowered, to deliver them from instant destruction.

John buries his face into his arm and pulls the lever. As the great drawbridge lowers slowly into place, John hears the agonizing cries of his son as the monstrous gear box breaks Greg's bones and grinds him to death. He hears his son scream out: 'Daddy! Daddy! Help me, Daddy!'

Painfully, John lifts his face and looks at the passengers aboard the train that his precious son has just given his life to save. Some read the daily newspaper, completely unaware of John. Others chat and drink coffee in the dining car, oblivious even to the crossing of the bridge. Some children laugh and play happily with trinkets and toys. Only a few passengers look John's way, extend their hand, and smile a heartfelt smile that says, 'Thank you.'

No one sees the tears on John's face. No one notices the small crushed body in the gear box below. And no one guesses the price just paid so that they might cross the river safely.

To most of the passengers aboard the Memphis Express, it's just another day, just another crossing.[1]

The Cost to God

When I first heard this true story of John Griffin and his son Greg, I felt like a nine-year-old girl again, sitting at my grandfather's feet, listening to him read from the big black Bible he held on his lap.

> 'For God so loved the world that He gave His only begotten Son....'

---

[1] I first heard this story told by Adolph Coors IV, *Shades Mountain Baptist Church*, 1991. (I have paraphrased it.)

'God love you so much, Nisey ....' Papa stopped reading to tell me, 'That He gave His only Son, Jesus ... that whoever believes in Him should not perish but have everlasting life' (John 3:16 (NKJV). He finished reading and then focused his sky-blue eyes on mine.

And that hot afternoon in August, the verse he read to me changed my life. Forever.

Truly, the privilege of prayer comes not without a great cost to the Father, a great cost to His Son.

Analogies can only go so far, but in many ways Greg's story reminds me of God's story – the story of Jesus' death on a cross.

For God, the Father, looked down on that warm spring day, 2000 years ago, and His heart stabbed with pain, His eyes filled with tears.

Oh, how He loved His boy, His only Son, arrested by soldiers, spit upon, and mocked. But there was only one thing to do. For a world of people were speeding through time and space, passing through the centuries, and they were depending on Him to save them from eternal destruction.

So the Father buried His face in His arm and allowed the executioner to hammer the nails into His Son's frail body. As the cross was lifted and lodged into the ground, God heard the agonizing cries of His Son. God heard the Son's screams: 'Daddy! Daddy! Why, Daddy?!' And on that day we call 'Good Friday,' Jesus hung by nailed hands and feet and died a slow death.

And the passengers abroad Planet Earth? Some read the daily newspaper ... others chatted and drank coffee in the dining car ... some children laughed and played happily with trinkets and toys. Only a few looked God's way, extended their hand, and smiled a heartfelt smile that said, 'Thank You.'

No one saw the tears on God's face. Few noticed or remembered the crushed bruised body upon that wooden cross. And no one guessed the price just paid so that they might cross the River safely.

To most of the passengers aboard Planet Earth, it was just another day, just another crossing.

While this story so aptly demonstrates God's love and Jesus' sacrifice, there is one huge difference. Little Greg's fall into the gear box was accidental. Death took Greg's life without his willing consent. Jesus, on the other hand, willingly offered His life for the world's lost people. And Jesus suffered more pain than just the agony of physical death. Humankind's sins were placed upon His shoulders that day, and He endured a death that no one ever has, or ever will experience again. An indescribably painful death. For you and for me.

The privilege to pray came at great cost to Jesus. Oh, that you and I will never allow this phenomenon of prayer to become a route to ritual, a lukewarm litany, or a half-hearted behest made as by a customer to an ecclesiastical bellhop! Prayer is too priceless, too precious, to be put off, to be unappreciated.

For the believer in Christ, prayer is the very beat of her heart, the next breath of air she will breathe, the center of her thoughts, desires, and deep affections. Prayer is the gift of Christ, Himself, a gift He willingly gives, a prize to cherish, an opportunity to extend our hands to Him. Slip out of Shadow-World and step into the presence of God Almighty – the One who loves us, the One who gave Himself for us, the One who, even now, prays for us.

The Holy Spirit – Our Teacher

'The One who, even now, prays for us....'

Insight visited me one early quiet morning as I sat in my secret place and waited in prayer. This never-before dawned insight has since given me new understanding in my prayer life. So simple yet so profound, so apparent yet so imperceptible, the insight is this: 'I do not know how to pray.'

The acknowledgment of such inability frightens me and terribly humbles me. For I am like a little child who stands before my heavenly Parent with selfish babblings and immature wants. I am a limited human being, a woman who truly loves the Lord and has given herself to Him, yet prayer lies so beyond my human capacity to understand, to faithfully and properly practice without help.

I am reminded of the difficult delivery of my first child, my only son, Christian. Two weeks overdue – hot August weeks – weeks that gave new meaning to the word 'waiting' – Christian was an impatient package of eager new life, yet unable to be born without help. So, to aid me with the birth, a skilled surgeon sliced open with ease my protruding abdomen, lifting from me that which I could not deliver alone. In doing so, the gifted helper gave my son 'wings' – the ability to breathe with his own lungs, the power to take on life that lived beyond me.

The analogy is a rather crude one, but prayer is somewhat like that C-Section I underwent 25 years ago. The prayers that live within my heart are like impatient packages of new life, eager to make themselves known to the Father. Yet, I need One greater than I, the gifted Helper, to deliver to God that which I cannot alone deliver. I need assistance to lift from me my heart's petitions and make them acceptable to approach the Almighty's ears.

Therefore ...

God provides One greater than I to teach me how to pray. God fills my whole being with Himself, the Holy Spirit, my Teacher, my Helper, my lifelong Guide. And I no longer pray with selfish babblings and immature wants. I pray a prayer with beauty and grace, a prayer uttered for me by the One who knows the heart of God, by the One who knows how to Pray, by the One who gives my prayers 'wings' so that they might live apart from me and so fill the Father's heart.

The Mystery of the Trinity

And when my prayers reach God's ears, He reaches out and wraps His gentle arms around me. For I am His, the one He loves, the child who takes her first awkward steps in pursuit of walking a lifetime in prayerful communion with Him.

Can you and I ever understand the mystery of the Trinity that enables us to pray?

Of God the Father, Who hears our prayers and Who responds to our petitions?

Of God the Son, Who willingly gave His life to reconcile us to the Father, and to grant us the privilege of prayer?

And of God the Holy Spirit Who helps us pray those prayers we cannot plead alone?

Such is the power of God the Father in our lives, redeeming us through God the Son, reforming us through God the Holy Spirit. God the Holy Spirit prays on our behalf to God the Father in the name of the One who made prayer possible, God the Son.

Deep calls unto deep, and I confess to you, the mystery of prayer is beyond my comprehension. I do not know how to pray. I will forever need the Helper to free within me those prayers that struggle to be born.

Perhaps the only prayer I can truly pray is the prayer of the publican in Luke 18:13. Like he, with bowed head and bowed heart, I beg: 'God, have mercy on me, a sinner.'

It's humbling, to be sure, but I believe this is the way to approach the Father, for this prayer is prayed without fear of an intruding arrogance or pride or self-righteousness. It is a prayer that can only be prayed with an appreciative heart, a grateful heart, a humble heart, for I owe God a debt that I can never repay.

I agree with D. T. Niles when he said we are all just beggars telling one another where to find bread.

How beautiful is the love of God that He so heartily embraces us beggars and envelops us with a love beyond the grasp of words to describe.

Priceless, Precious Prayer

So it is with first-step clumsiness, a mere toddler's try at walking, that I lift my heart and open it wide, giving God my love, receiving His love, and with the Holy Spirit's help, I approach my Father in prayer.

And I discover anew ...

The prayer of the waiting heart, the prayer that cannot be rushed, the prayer that needs time to think, to ponder, to brood, to watch, to listen. The prayer that 'stands under in active strength enduring till the answer comes.'

The prayer of the struggling heart, the prayer that falls on bended knee to the Creator of all humankind, beseeching, pleading, begging on behalf of the world's unknown others who hurt and hunger and sorrow and grieve, the world's little lambs who have yet to respond to the loving Shepherd's heart.

The prayer of the expectant heart, the prayer that waits on tiptoe, wide-eyed and curious, expecting a surprise from the One Who whispers when we expect Him to shout, from the One Who shouts when we expect Him to whisper.

The prayer of the prepared heart, the prayer that keeps praying while riding 'round and 'round the merry-go-round of life. The prayer that listens always for the Father's voice amidst the chaos and noise and confusion of Shadow-World society.

The prayer of the servant's heart, the prayer that prays by name and need, the prayer that intercedes for those whose faces grace the bedside wall.

The prayer of the Shepherd's heart, the prayer Christ prays on our behalf, the gift of prayer that Christ purchased for you, for me, on a warm spring day on a wooden cross.

Priceless, precious prayer is a secret, yours and mine, to be enjoyed, to be planned, to be anticipated, throughout our days, throughout our lives. For our hours of solitude, our still hours, are sacred hours, not to be spent carelessly, but to be used carefully, to be cherished, sought, savored, shared.

How ironic that you and I, as believers in Christ, seek the solitude that society shuns, pursue the silence from which humankind runs to escape, embrace the aloneness from which the world flees and labels loneliness.

Share the secret.

Solitude, silence, aloneness – so vital to, so treasured by, the one who prays; so strange, so frightening to the one who doesn't, to the one who strays.

There are so many ways to pray. So many ways to fellowship with our Father. The ways to pray are as distinctive as you and I, a world of Christ-devoted women with personalities and talents so beautifully varied. Yet, we each hold dear the secret that makes us sisters – our 'yes' to the Shepherd's love, our response to the Shepherd's sacrifice, our closeness to the Shepherd's heart.

Prayer – wonderful, beautiful prayer ... what a gift, what a privilege!

Sometimes I need to sing and dance and clap my hands as David did when he offered his prayers of thanksgiving to God before the Ark of the Lord.[2] How often can my body speak the language of joy unknown to rigid words.

Sometimes I need to feel the hurt that cuts my heart in two, to cry the tears God saves of mine, to let my prayer be one of pain, a pain too deep for words.

Sometimes I need to walk again the road that leads to Calvary, to pray my words of gratitude. Yet I need words so

2. 2 Samuel 6:14.

lovely to the ear, so rich to the heart, that language, itself, does not contain them. So my heart must speak within itself those words not yet discovered.

Surely, my heart yearns for that which I cannot put into words, that which my limited language cannot express. Otherwise, how shallow my prayers would be if they were restricted to the concrete walls of my imprisoned vocabulary. The prayer from the very depths of my heart is a prayer unspeakable, a prayer full of thanks and joy, dance and tears, song and sorrow.

Surely the gift of prayer is so full of potential and promise, so blessed by a woman's unique individual expression, the Holy Spirit will never allow it to settle into predictable patterns.

Our prayers must take on the newness that each morning brings to our Christ-devoted hearts. For each day is presented to us pregnant with surprise, expectation, and discovery. Just as the old Indian once placed his foot in a river's stream, he could not place it there again within the stream's same spot.

So ... today in prayer we dance and sing, tomorrow we sigh and cry. Each day blesses us singularly, for the river never ceases to flow and times leaves us standing each day within a different stream.

> But thou, when thou prayest, enter into thy closet, and when thou hast shut thy door, pray to thy Father which is in secret (Matt. 6:6 KJV).

When I hear that verse, I remember Mama, my beloved grandmother, for Mama spent much time in her closet secreted with the Father. In fact, her entire life was prayer.

Surely every heart must have its hush, to wait and listen in sacred solitude, to go out and stand on the mountaintop, to 'be still and know that I am God.'

More than anyone else, Mama taught me the value and beauty of a secret place and a prayer of waiting and listening to the still, small voice that whispers within the prayer-closet walls.

Oh that I could know God like Elijah and Mama knew Him!

Jesus, Elijah and Moses

We meet Elijah one more time before the scriptures close his story. He stands again on a mountaintop, this time with Jesus and Moses. The mountains are not unknown by these three men, for they have spent much time upon the hills in prayer.

Three disciples, Peter, James, and John, watch and rub their eyes in disbelief when Jesus' robes become white with blinding light, and there appear with Him two prophets from the past.

'Please stay,' the disciples urge, and they offer to build houses where they might dwell.

But years ago, Moses had to leave the mountaintop to deliver tables of stone.

Years ago, Elijah, too, had to climb down and stand at the mouth of the cave, awaiting instructions from God for the work he was to do.

For their waiting hearts had heard the Whisper, and their listening hearts were changed and opened and eager to obey.

And now, you disciples, Peter, James, and John. Jesus cannot stay upon the mountaintop either. He cannot accept your offer of lodging. For the world's stray lambs are lost in a thicket dense and the Shepherd must go to rescue His flock and save them from the dark night's wolves.

For once we hear God's gentle whisper, we can no longer remain on the mountaintop. We must come down, and we must obey.

Questions for Group Study

1. What verse of Scripture is most meaningful to you? Share the scripture with the group.

2. 'Truly, the privilege of prayer comes not without a great cost to the Father, a great cost to His Son.'

   a. Silently ponder the great price paid by the Father and the Son for our salvation.

    b. Offer God a heartfelt prayer of gratitude as you reflect on His love and His sacrifice for you.

3. What is meant by the following statement: 'I do not know how to pray.' Do you find it to be true in your own life? Why or why not?

4. Reread this statement and respond as a group to its meaning: 'God the Holy Spirit prays on our behalf to God the Father in the name of the One who made prayer possible, God the Son.'

5. Meditate on the words of D. T. Niles: 'We are all just beggars telling one another where to find bread.'

    a. Do you agree or disagree, and why?

    b. What does this image say to you? Please explain.

6. One by one, examine the following type of prayers, and explain what each means to your own personal prayer life:

    a. The prayer of the waiting heart
    b. The prayer of the struggling heart
    c. The prayer of the expectant heart
    d. The prayer of the prepared heart
    e. The prayer of the servant's heart
    f. The prayer of the Shepherd's heart

7. What are some of the ways you find most meaningful to pray? If time permits, name them and discuss them as a group.

8. Read Romans 8:26-27 and discuss this question: What is the work of the Holy Spirit in our prayers, in our lives?

Suggestions for Personal Reflection

· Read 1 Corinthians 4:7 and James 1:17. Contemplate their meanings. Why is it essential that we pray special prayers of thanksgiving to God for the gifts He has given us? Why should we

    · Thank Him for those gifts for which we are most grateful?

- · Distinguish within ourselves those gifts that are temporary and those gifts that are eternal?
- · Pray that we can receive, use, and give to others those gifts He gives to us?

· Read John 14:26, 16:8, and Romans 8:9. Ask God to grant you keener understanding of His Holy spirit as He works in your life. Plan a special time of devotions and reflect on your personal experience with Jesus Christ. Ask yourself these questions:

- · Have I become a new creature since I gave my life to the Lord? In what ways have I changed? In what ways do I need to change?
- · How can regular and frequent prayer transform me to the image of Christ? How can I better follow the example of prayer Jesus taught in Scripture?
- · How can frequent prayer protect me from the Evil One? How can I become less vulnerable to Satan and to temptation by staying close to God in prayer? (Read Prov. 4:14-15; Matt. 26:41; 1 Cor. 10:13; Heb. 12:1; James 1:12-15; 1 John 5:18-19.)

· Read and ponder the words of praise offered by David in 1 Chronicles 29:10-13. How does David's act of praise speak to you in regard to personal worship?

· Read Revelation 5:13; 11:15. Contemplate the eternal kingdom, power, and glory of the Lord as you reflect upon those verses.

For Deeper Understanding of Scripture

1. For scriptures regarding the Trinity, read Genesis 1:2; Deuteronomy 6:4; Psalm 33:6, 9, 104:30, 107:20; Proverbs 3:19, 8:1-36; John 1:1-4; and Zechariah 4:6.

   a. Also read Matthew 3:3-17, 28:19; Mark 1:9-11; Luke 3:21-22; John 14:16, 15:26, 16:13-15; 1 Corinthians 12:3-6; 2 Corinthians 13:14; Galatians 4:4-6; Ephesians 4:4-6; 1 Peter 1:2; and Revelation 1:4.

   b. Then using the Scripture references above, please respond to the following four statements:

      i. God is One.
      ii. God has three distinct ways of being in the redemptive event, however He remains an undivided unity.
      iii. We can grasp the concept of the Trinity through the threefold participation in salvation.
      iv. The Trinity is a mystery we cannot adequately explain or, with our human minds, fully understand.

   c. Discuss the role the Trinity plays in our prayers today.

2. Who is Jesus Christ, and what is the significance of

    a. His preexistence (see John 1:1)

    b. His conception and birth (see the beginning chapters of Matthew and Luke)

    c. His crucifixion, death, and burial (see Luke 23:50-56; John 19:38-42; Acts 1-12; and Gal. 3)

    d. His resurrection (see Matt. 27:56, 61; 28:1-2, 16-20; Mark 16; Luke 24:13-32, 34, 36-43; John 20:11-18, 24-29; Acts 9:1-9; and 1 Cor. 15:3-8)

    e. Ponder the following: where is Jesus Christ now, and what is His work in regards to our lives, to our prayer lives? (See Matt. 26:64; Mark 14:62; and Luke 22:69)

3. Read 2 Timothy 3:16 and describe the work of the Holy Spirit in the Bible.

    a. What role does the Holy Spirit take as far as helping us to understand the Scriptures and their deeper meaning and implications?

    b. Regarding the Bible today, do you agree with this statement, and why or why not: "The Bible has no rival in its pervasive influence upon Western culture, and increasingly over world culture?"

    c. What do you see as the role and the importance of the Bible in today's society/world?

4. Using only the parables of Jesus, describe the conversion experience that redeems us and guarantees us life everlasting:

    a. Sin (see Matt. 22:2-9 and Luke 14:16-23, *The Marriage Supper*)

    b. Jesus Christ (see Luke 10:1-16, *The Good Samaritan*)

    c. Conviction (see Luke 7:41, *The Prayer of the Convicted*)

    d. Repentance (see Matt. 7:14 and Luke 13:24, *The Narrow Gate*)

    e. God's forgiveness (see Matt. 18:23-25, *Two Debtors*)

    f. Perseverance in prayer (see Luke 18:2-5, *The Widow*)

    g. Humility in prayer (see Luke 18:10-14, *The Pharisee and the Tax-Gatherer*)

More About Elijah

We can learn a lot today about God by studying God's prophet, Elijah.

Elijah's world – almost a thousand years before Jesus was born – was as dangerous and unsafe as our world today. Constant war killed people and destroyed property. His world in 875 BC was as violent and unstable as our world is today. It was also a wicked and evil time. In fact, Elijah lived in Israel's Northern Kingdom – the very area where Hezbollah (in Lebanon) and Israel were just recently bombing each other.

First Kings begins with Solomon's succession to the throne, his request for God's wisdom and the construction of the Temple. It should have been a time of peace and prosperity, a time when Israel worshipped the one true God – the God of Abraham and Moses and David.

But, as wise as Solomon was, he did some stupid things that caused Israel to decline and deteriorate and to turn away from God.

First of all, Solomon imposed a heavy tax on his people. Their own hard-earned money paid for Solomon's many elaborate building projects.

Second, Solomon used forced slave labor to construct his buildings. The people were forced to work. (Years later, when Solomon died and his son became king, they begged him to 'lighten the harsh labor and the heavy yoke that his father, Solomon, had put on them.' His answer: 'My father laid on you a heavy yoke; I will make it even heavier. My father scourged you with whips; I will scourge you with scorpions.')

Third, Solomon married many pagan women, and he foolishly allowed his pagan wives to draw him into idol worship. Solomon led all of Israel to worship false gods: storm gods, sun-moon-war-water-and-grain-gods. Israel became spiritually-confused. And remember, it was Solomon who once wrote: 'The fear of the LORD is the beginning of wisdom, and knowledge of the Holy One is understanding' (Prov. 9:10). Yet he, himself, fell away from God. (We see this happening in our own day with Christians incorporating false beliefs into their Christian worship practices – beliefs drawn from New Age, Wicca, astrology/horoscopes, communicating with the dead, and other pagan practices.)

When Solomon died, the nation of Israel split apart, causing tension, war, instability, and hardship between Israel and Judah. People moved far away from worshipping the true God, and continued to worship 'golden calves' and 'pagan gods.' The book of 1 Kings lists king after evil king who continued to lead Israel away from God. When wicked Ahab became king, his evil wife, Queen Jezebel, introduced yet another false god – Baal – supposedly 'the god of fertility and lord of the rain clouds.' It was a time of chaos and crisis. Not much different than the world today.

That's when Elijah came on the scene. He was God's prophet. His job was to turn the people back to God and covenant faithfulness. Not an easy task.

Elijah was from Tishbe in the Northern Kingdom – a 'Tishbite.' Tishbe was located about half way between the Sea of Galilee and the Dead Sea.

Elijah's divine assignment was to confront King Ahab. Scripture tells us that Ahab 'did more evil in the eyes of the Lord than any of those [kings] before him.' Jezebel was just as evil. She rounded up God's prophets and killed them. She formed her own group of prophets – four hundred and fifty false prophets who worshipped Baal.

But God loved Israel. No matter how disobedient they were, He continued to love them. He would not let them go.

Later, the apostle Paul would write about God's strong possessive love:

> Who shall separate us from the love of Christ? ... I am convinced that neither death nor life, neither angels nor demons, neither the present nor the future, nor any powers, neither height nor depth, nor anything else in all creation, will be able to separate us from the love of God that is in Christ Jesus our Lord.' We might add: 'neither Ahab or Baal or Jezebel can separate us from the love of God (Rom. 8:38).

God sent Elijah to Ahab with this message: 'As the LORD, the God of Israel, lives, whom I serve, there will be neither dew nor rain in the next few years except at my word.' The rain stopped, and the ground dried up. God sent Elijah to the east of the Jordan to a little brook of fresh water. He sent ravens to feed him there.

Why did God stop the rain? To mock the false god, Baal. You see, Baal was supposed to be the god of fertility and the lord of the rain clouds. The rain stopped, and nothing grew. No doubt, the people prayed day and night to Baal to do his job – to send rain and make the crops grow. God showed his people that Baal was powerless.

But God takes care of those who love and obey Him. When Elijah's little brook dried up, God led Elijah to the home of a pagan widow who fed him. When the widow's son became sick and died, Elijah brought him back to life, causing the widow to worship the true God.

After several years of drought, God told Elijah: 'Go and present yourself to Ahab, and I will send rain on the land. So Elijah went to present himself to Ahab.'

When Ahab and Elijah came face to face, Ahab said: 'Is that you, you troubler of Israel?'

'I have not made trouble for Israel,' Elijah replied. 'But you and your father's family have. You have abandoned the LORD's commands and have followed the Baals.' Then Elijah challenged Ahab: 'Now summon the people from all over Israel to meet me on Mount Carmel. And bring the four hundred and fifty false prophets of Baal.'

So Ahab sent word throughout all Israel and assembled the prophets of Baal on Mount Carmel. It was SHOWDOWN time! What happened next was amazing!

(Let's hear what happened from Elijah, himself.)

There they were – all the phony Baal prophets gathered on Mt. Carmel. This was it – once and for all God wanted to show the wicked people that He was the one True God – not Baal, the false god who 'rode the thunderstorm in his divine chariots and spoke with thunder and killed with lightning.'

I faced them all and then hollered out: 'How long will you people waver between two opinions? If the LORD is God, follow Him; but if Baal is God, follow him.'

Nobody said anything.

So I shouted: 'I am the only one of the LORD's prophets left, but Baal has four hundred and fifty prophets!'

I told them to bring me two bulls – one for Baal and one for the LORD.

'Cut it into pieces and put it on the wood,' I told them. I did the same thing with the other bull.

'Call on the name of your god, Baal,' I shouted, 'And I will call on the name of the LORD. The god who answers by fire – he is God.'

'Okay! That's good!' the people shouted back at me.

Those poor false prophets screamed out to Baal from morning till noon. They cried: 'O Baal, answer us!' They danced around the altar they had made, and begged Baal to send down fire to burn up the bull.

That's when I saw my chance to taunt them a little. 'Shout louder!' I told them. 'Surely he is a god. Perhaps he's deep in thought, or busy, or traveling or asleep. Wake him up!'

That really irked them. So they called louder to Baal, and they danced harder. Trying to arouse Baal, they took sharp stones and scraped the skin off their forearms. Then they took razors and cut up their faces. They slashed themselves with swords and spears and their blood flowed past midday. By evening, they had heard nothing from Baal.

Now it was my turn – God's turn! 'Come over here!' I called to the people. I took twelve stones, one for each of Israel's tribes. I rebuilt the altar 'in the name of the LORD,' and I dug a trench around it. I piled up the wood, cut up the bull, and laid it on the wood. Then I told them to fill four large jars with water and pour it over the bull and wood. After that, I told them to do it again, and then a third time. Everything was soaked. The water ran down around the altar and filled the trench.

Then I stepped forward and prayed out loud so everyone could hear: 'O LORD,' I prayed, 'God of Abraham, Isaac and Israel, let it be known today that YOU ARE GOD in Israel and that I am your servant and have done all these things at your command.' Then I shouted: 'Answer me, O LORD, answer me, so these people will know that you, O LORD, are God, and that you are turning their hearts back again.'

All of a sudden, fire came from heaven and burned up the bull, the wood, the stones, the soil, and even licked up the water in the trench! It was a sight to behold! It scared the people so much, they fell on their faces and cried out together: 'The LORD – He is God! The LORD – He is God!'

Then the prophets of Baal were caught and slaughtered.

God is all-powerful. Just like Elijah, we can trust Him because He is the One true Creator and Sustainer of all the universe. On Mt. Carmel that night, there was no doubt in anyone's mind that God was the One True God.

That night, after the showdown on Mt. Carmel, Elijah was feeling very brave, courageous, and victorious. God finally ended the drought and sent rain to Israel. But then Ahab went home and told Jezebel everything Elijah had done – including how he had killed all her false prophets. Jezebel was furious!

That's when Elijah got scared. He could stand up to four hundred and fifty false prophets, but Jezebel was a different story. So Elijah ran away. In fact, he ran as far as he could – all the way to the edge of Judah – to the wilderness of Beersheba. Then he just gave up. 'I've had enough, LORD,' he whined. Then a depressed Elijah sat down under a broom tree and prayed that he might die.

But again, God took care of Elijah – even out there in the harsh wilderness of Beersheba. God sent His angel twice to Elijah with baked bread and a jar of water. Elijah ate, drank, and rested. Then he felt strong enough to travel forty days and nights till he reached Horeb (or Mt. Sinai) – a good 250 miles south of Beersheba. [Mt. Sinai was the mountain where God had given Moses the ten commandments on stone tablets. It was called 'the mountain of God.'] Elijah went into a cave and spent the night. That's where the LORD appeared to Elijah – and again Elijah whined: 'I have been very zealous for the LORD God Almighty. The Israelites have rejected your covenant, broken down your altars, and put your prophets to death with the sword. I am the only one left, and now they are trying to kill me too.'

Elijah had forgotten the power of the LORD, how He had dried up the rain clouds and then ended the drought; how He had sent fire from heaven and burned up the offering, altar, wood, stones, soil, and water; how He had protected Elijah from wicked Jezebel and had sent an angel to feed the hungry prophet. Now he was worried, upset, crying and whining – 'They're gonna kill me too, LORD!' he cried.

That's when the LORD spoke to Elijah again: 'Go out and stand on the mountain in the presence of the LORD,' God told him, 'for the LORD is about to pass by.'

Elijah went out and stood on the mountain and waited for God to speak. Then a great and powerful wind tore the mountains apart and shattered the rocks before the LORD. After the wind, came a powerful earthquake. After the earthquake came a fire. But God didn't speak through the wind. And God didn't speak through the earthquake. And God didn't speak through the fire. God came to a terrified whining scared Elijah in 'a gentle whisper.' Scripture tells us that when Elijah heard it, he pulled his cloak over his face and went out and stood at the mouth of the cave. And that's when God gave Elijah his new marching orders, and encouraged, Elijah obeyed.

Isn't it interesting how we sometimes expect God to come to us in a dramatic, Mt. Sinai-kind-of-way, and instead He speaks to us in an ordinary, everyday 'quiet whisper'? Fortunately, Elijah was watching and listening, and when God gently whispered to him, he heard.

God told Elijah to take another message to Ahab. Did Elijah want to face Ahab and Jezebel? NO! In fact, Ahab and Jezebel had recently murdered an innocent landowner, Naboth, so they could seize his property. Elijah had to stand before the two murderers and tell them that God had judged them and they would both die. (Not a popular, or a pretty, message!) Ahab repented, lived a while longer, and then died a violent death in a battle.

And Jezebel? She was thrown from a window in Jezreel. As she fell, some of her blood spattered the wall. Then the horses trampled her to death. Before she could be scooped up and buried, dogs ate her flesh and licked her blood. (These weren't cute little Cocker Spaniels or dainty-dolled-up French Poodles. These dogs were wild and vicious and frightening.) The dogs left nothing to bury, but her skull, feet, and hands. Just like Elijah had told her.

God keeps His promises.

And what happened to Elijah? One day Elijah and his successor, Elisha, were walking and talking when suddenly a <u>chariot of fire and horses of fire</u> appeared and took Elijah up to heaven in a whirlwind!' What a way to go!!!

But we meet Elijah again – in Matthew 17:1-8: the transfiguration of Jesus. 'After six days Jesus took with him Peter, James and John ... and led them up a high mountain by themselves. There he was transfigured before them, His face shone like the sun, and His clothes became as white as the light. Just then there appeared before them Moses and *Elijah*, talking with Jesus.'

And when John the Baptist was born, people thought John was really Elijah coming back to them (Matt. 17:9-13). Jesus tells his disciples that: 'To be sure, Elijah comes and will restore all things ... and the disciples understood that he was talking about John the Baptist.'

We also hear about Elijah in the last book of the Old Testament, Malachi 4:5-6 – the very last verse. The prophet Malachi writes God's words: 'See, I will send you the prophet *Elijah* before that great and dreadful day of the LORD comes. He will turn the hearts of the fathers to their children, and the hearts of the children to their fathers; or else I will come and strike the land with a curse.'

What can you and I learn from the prophet Elijah – who lived and worked almost 3,000 years ago?

1. We can trust with certainty that God is in control. Even when Israel bombs Lebanon and Lebanon bombs Israel; and even when terrorists threaten to blow up trans-Atlantic jets, God is still in control. Nothing happens in this world that He doesn't, for some reason, allow to happen. And when tragedy DOES happen, Paul tells us that 'we know that in all things God works for the good of those who love him, who have been

called according to his purpose' (Rom. 8:28). Elijah learned that nothing can happen to us that God doesn't allow to happen, and if He allows us a crisis, He will work it for our good.

2. We can also know, like Elijah discovered, God is all-powerful. He can cause drought, and He can send rain. He can send fire from heaven to consume offerings and altars; and He can raise a widow's dead son back to life again. God is all-powerful. Nothing is beyond God's ability and power.

3. God can use Elijah to work and witness for Him, and God can use you and me to work and witness for Him. God used Elijah to face an evil king Ahab, and to stand before pagan prophets. God has a unique purpose for you and me, too. Scripture tells us 'When I was woven together in the depths of the earth, your eyes saw my unformed body. All the days ordained for me were written in your book before one of them came to be' (Ps. 139).

4. God hears the individual cries of His prophets and His children. When Elijah cried out to God (in his fear of Jezebel), God heard him. And God comforted Elijah with the shade of a broom tree, and with angels bearing food and drink. The Psalmist writes (in Ps. 145): 'The LORD is righteous in all his ways and loving toward all he has made. The LORD is near to all who call on him, to all who call on him in truth ... the LORD watches over all who love him....'

5. And lastly, Elijah teaches us that when we get scared, tuck our tails between our legs, and run to far-away Beersheba, God doesn't kick us out of His kingdom's work. When we fail Him, He forgives us, He cares for us, He gets us back on our feet, and, with a gentle encouraging whisper, He gives us new assignments – that we can accomplish for Him. God is the God of a second chance ... and a third chance, too!

CHRISTIAN FOCUS PUBLICATIONS
publishes books for all ages

Our mission statement –

STAYING FAITHFUL

In dependence upon God we seek to help make His infallible Word, the Bible, relevant. Our aim is to ensure that the Lord Jesus Christ is presented as the only hope to obtain forgiveness of sin, live a useful life and look forward to heaven with Him.

REACHING OUT
Christ's last command requires us to reach out to our world with His gospel. We seek to help fulfill that by publishing books that point people towards Jesus and help them develop a Christ-like maturity. We aim to equip all levels of readers for life, work, ministry and mission.

Books in our adult range are published in three imprints.
Christian Focus contains popular works including biographies, commentaries, basic doctrine and Christian living. Our children's books are also published in this imprint.
Mentor focuses on books written at a level suitable for Bible College and seminary students, pastors, and other serious readers. The imprint includes commentaries, doctrinal studies, examination of current issues and church history.
Christian Heritage contains classic writings from the past.

Christian Focus Publications, Ltd
Geanies House, Fearn, Ross-shire,
IV20 1TW, Scotland, United Kingdom
info@christianfocus.com

For details of our titles visit us on our website
www.christianfocus.com